THE HIGH PERFORMANCE MINDSET

Carter!

A strong mind
will overcome a strong body +
a strong mind is
where it is at!

THE HIGH PERFORMANCE MINDSET

A FRAMEWORK FOR SUCCESS IN BUSINESS, SPORTS, AND LIFE

CRAIG WILLARD

LIONCREST
PUBLISHING

THE HIGH PERFORMANCE MINDSET
A Framework for Success in Business, Sports, and Life

ISBN 978-1-61961-732-2 *Paperback*
      978-1-61961-733-9 *Ebook*

CONTENTS

ACKNOWLEDGMENTS

I am so grateful to have the opportunity to make a difference in this world.

This wouldn't be possible, though, without my parents, Joanie Doll and Steve Willard. I love you both and thank you for helping me to become the person I am today.

My daughter, Ashlyn, you are my world and inspire me every day to be better; your patience with me as I took time out of my day to work on this book has helped me stay the course. Daddy loves you.

To my sister, Lauren Doll, thanks for supporting my every move; I love you.

To my stepdad, Pat Doll, who has shown a tremendous amount of support to my mother and sister through some of the toughest years. Thank you for being such an influence in my life. I love you!

To my friend, Brad Wands, thank you for the support you have given me through my journey and for the support in writing this book. When I first came to you about writing this book, you didn't even hesitate when I mentioned it. "Go for it!" you said.

To Jay Bates, one of my closest friends who has been an unrelenting supporter of everything I have ever done and constantly reminds me that I can do anything.

And, to all the people I've been blessed to get to know. You have shaped my life and helped me to become the person I am today. While I may not have included your name, I thank you.

And, to you, the person who has purchased this book. I tip my hat to you and I am proud of you!

INTRODUCTION

Is this for me?

I bet that's what you're asking yourself. Is the high performance mindset for me?

Let's talk about you. You're probably an intelligent person who works hard, takes care of yourself and the people around you, and has achieved a level of success that would satisfy most people. However, you're not "most people." You want more—a lot more out of your life—you just don't know how to get it.

So, is the high performance mindset for you? If any of the statements below describes you, the answer is: Absolutely!

- You're an entrepreneur, executive, athlete, or student looking to achieve phenomenal levels of success.
- There's something in your way, perhaps an invisible barrier that you can't seem to find. This barrier seems to hold you back from achieving success in your career, in sports, or in your relationships.
- You keep getting things you don't want in your life, while things you do want are always beyond your reach.
- You feel stuck in a rut, like your life's a repetitive cycle that's going nowhere.

First and foremost, I commend you for picking up this book, because doing so is a clear sign that you're motivated to do great things with your life. That's where your mindset comes in. Taking this first step shows that your mindset is already bending toward what's possible. Although you may not even be aware of it, your mind is capable of creating a better, happier, and more fulfilled life.

Many people will never take this step. It's easy to be complacent and settle for where you are and what you have in life. The main reason for this is that most people don't know—from a psychological perspective—how they got to where they are right now. More importantly, they don't know what to do about it. Why do so many people get stuck in a low-performing rut, struggling to get ahead?

And why do so many high performers get to a certain level in life and then seem to hit a brick wall? You may have to go back many, many years to discover the answer to that question. However, we'll discuss what you can do about it soon!

Your mindset began to evolve when you were very young and while it has changed over time, beliefs established during your childhood linger in your adult mind and keep you from reaching your full potential. Becoming aware of these limitations is essential to overcoming them and developing the high performance mindset. These beliefs may have worked for you when you were younger; however, they don't work for you anymore and operating with an outdated mindset can prevent you from achieving everything you want in life: love, a great career, personal goals, success, and even happiness. Despite these lingering, limiting beliefs, many people go on to become happy, successful adults. However, they know they can do more. They *want* to do more. The high performance mindset benefits anyone who wants more out of life. It's a mindset you can develop using a concrete set of techniques that have a firm foundation in psychology and have been put to work in the real world. I put them together, I tested them, and I know they work.

Full disclosure: Who am *I* to tell *you* about the high

performance mindset? I'm the last person you'd expect. I'm a guy from a small town in Kentucky who graduated eighth in his class...from the bottom! That's right; I graduated from high school at 172 out of 179 students, with a whopping 1.448 GPA. How I got from *there* to where I am *today*—an entrepreneur, high performance coach, and author who has guided executives, athletes, and everyday people to new heights in their careers, sports, and personal lives—is a result of what I am about to teach you.

I've spent years putting this together: reading, learning, developing mindset techniques, applying them to myself and to my clients, and studying the results. It took a lot of work to develop and hone these techniques because the research behind them can be complicated. I believe that's why so few people have had the opportunity to develop a high performance mindset. It seems complicated. However, once I boiled down the psychology to its core principles, I knew I could present this in a format you could learn and apply without a psychology background. Inspired by the possibilities, I developed simple tools that delivered powerful, consistent results. That, in turn, inspired me to write this book and share my knowledge with you. Anyone can do this. Discovering your best life shouldn't be complicated, and it isn't if you follow the instructions I've laid out for you in this book.

In my research as a student, a coach, and a leader, I discovered that many of the same life and sports psychology tools that empower professional athletes to outperform their competitors on the field, on the track, and in the ring can empower executives, entrepreneurs, and people just like you to create a better, fuller life. These tools help you remove self-doubt and uncover more confidence. They also help you build better relationships. The core principles presented in the high performance mindset techniques are based on sports psychology and cognitive behavioral coaching and are transferable across a broad range of professional and personal goals. They work fast and are extremely effective.

Let's do a quick rewind, though. I want to tell you about my personal journey to entrepreneur, coach, and author. My life didn't follow a traditional path and neither did my success. There's a path that most people have been conditioned to take: You go to school, get good grades, and go to college. You graduate and land a great career. Then you get married and start a family. That path sounds familiar, doesn't it? That path isn't for everyone, and it wasn't for me. First, I didn't care much for school. I was bored. To this day, I'm not necessarily a fan of the traditional style of teaching. It didn't work well for me. I wasn't interested in college or starting a career when I graduated high school, so I took odd jobs here and there. Eventually, I knew that if I wanted to achieve certain things in life I'd have to over-come some challenges. Back then, although I wasn't sure what those challenges were, I was committed to figuring them out, so that's what I focused on. The ability to see each obstacle in life as an opportunity or challenge to learn, improve, and progress turned out to be a key element in my personal development and an important concept in the high performance mindset.

My first challenge would be changing my own beliefs about myself. You might think it's impossible for people to change their beliefs, however, it is possible. I'll tell you how and why you should do it in Part I, **Chapter 1,** "What Is a High Performance Mindset?" and **Chapter 2,** "The Ever-Evolving Mind."

In my 20s, I discovered another challenge that, at the time, appeared to hold me back. I was diagnosed with general anxiety disorder. When you're anxious, you can't perform at your full potential. Anxiety was tough. It created a lot of problems in my life—or so I thought. I was put on a very strong prescription medication to help me cope with the anxiety. Essentially, the medication took away my lows, and it took away my highs, too. I felt like I was experiencing the world through a dirty filter, and I didn't enjoy that feeling at all. During this time, I was going to lunch daily with two buddies. The anti-anxiety medication took the life out of me, and they noticed—and were worried. I remember them saying to me, "You have to snap out of it!" I wanted to snap out of it; I felt isolated, as if I was living in a virtual cocoon separating me from the rest of the world. I was numb!

I made a decision to take massive action to stick with my prescription until the bottle was empty and then take myself off the meds. When I swallowed that last pill, I quit cold turkey! This turned out to be a huge mistake, because I then started feeling like I was going insane. No, seriously! I remember calling my doctor and begging him to help me make the feeling stop. Luckily, he had a sample pack of five pills at his office that he could give me. I started taking the meds again. Whew, what a relief! I returned to my "medicated state" determined to get off the medication the right way. This time, I slowly weaned myself off of it. In the meantime, I had to figure out how to manage the so-called "general anxiety disorder" I had been diagnosed with, without medication.

I did a lot of research and discovered the drugs weren't treating the actual cause of my anxiety at all. Instead, they were only treating the effects such as my restlessness, irritability, and the racing thoughts in my head. Honestly, I could have been on that medication for years and not gotten any better. In order to free myself from the constraints of anxiety and put myself in a better place, I needed to figure out the *cause* of my problem and fix it—once and for all! And guess what? I did it. I learned how to treat anxiety without drugs and I've been anxiety-free ever since—true story!

Decreasing and even eliminating anxiety became another core concept of the high performance mindset. In **Chapter 3**, "Understanding Your Mindset," I'll explain how the conscious mind and the subconscious mind interact to create your mindset, and why treating the effects of anxiety and depression with drugs can be an ineffective short-term solution. I'll also discuss linguistics—the words you use and your understanding of those words—and how it affects your thinking. The first exercise in that chapter will help you prove to yourself the power—and sometimes confusion—of linguistics, and a second exercise will teach you about multitasking. This is a big chapter so take your time, read each section, and follow along with the exercises and the diagrams. It's critical that you understand the concepts illustrated in Diagrams 1, 2, and 3 in order to fully appreciate the power of the high performance mindset—specifically, how and why it works. In **Chapter 4**, "Time and the Mind: Depression, Anxiety, and Happiness," you'll learn why the way your mind processes time can lead to anxiety and depression, and I'll show you how to process it a different way that unlocks the happier you. By the way, all the exercises in this book can also be found at http://www.thehighperformancemindset.net password THPM.

Fast-forward into my 30s, when I became a single father and was working in the IT department at the local hospital. I found myself wanting a better life for myself and my daughter. One day, one of the hospital executives asked me where I was going in my career. He said, "You can do ANYTHING you want. What do *you* want, Craig?" When I told him I wanted to become the next director of IT, he asked, "Well, how are you going to get there? You don't have a college degree and that will become a barrier for you," and he was right. I'd been figuring things out on my own my whole life. I would literally apply for positions that I had no clue how to fulfill, knowing that if I got the opportunity to sit in the seat, I'd figure out how to do the job. However, let's be honest: I needed a formal education to be considered for the director position. I needed to figure out how I—a guy who had never even *considered* going to college—was going to get my college degree *and* do it as a single parent with a full-time position. I could have told myself that I didn't have time as a single parent. I could have worried about my 1.448 GPA. I could have told myself I wasn't smart enough for college; however, I knew that wasn't true because, by then, I'd figured out that I could always learn and grow. I could stop thinking of myself as "not smart enough" and realize I *was* smart enough. I overcame my self-defeating thoughts—and so can you!

How do you banish self-defeating thoughts? It starts with learning to control your thoughts while dealing with irrational, negative thoughts that ultimately hold you back. The most effective method I've found for dealing with and removing negative thoughts is called *rational emotive behavioral coaching,* or REBC, which was developed by psychologist Dr. Albert Ellis. Applying REBC to your thoughts and beliefs empowers you to question their validity and determine if they're true or false, rational or irrational. You might be surprised that many truths you tell yourself aren't true at all! In **Chapter 5,** "Dealing with Negative and Self-Defeating Thoughts," I'll show you how you can dispel negative thoughts and replace them with positive thinking that takes your life in a new direction. By learning how to deal with my negative and self-defeating thoughts, I was able to go to college, earn a bachelor's degree and an MBA, and become the director of the IT department.

Fast-forward a few more years when, as the IT director, I was working on developmental goals and performance management plans with my staff. I quickly realized that I wasn't trained to give my people the direction and plans they truly deserved. I felt like I was cheating my staff.

Although I wanted to coach them, help them set goals, and teach them how to achieve these goals, I didn't know how. I asked my senior director at the time if he would be willing to pay for training so that I could effectively help my staff. He wasn't very receptive to my request, and I knew I couldn't wait around for my company to teach me performance management and developmental goal setting, so I enrolled in coaching classes on my own. This step ultimately changed the trajectory of my whole life. I learned how to coach my staff, and I also learned a more important lesson that changed my life.

Coaching taught me that when you do things for other people, it comes back to you. The more you give, the more you get in return. I felt like I'd stumbled on life's most precious principle. In fact, this concept is very much the keystone to a happy and fulfilled life.

I started coaching on the side, first working as a life coach and then coaching triathletes all over the country. This experience opened a new world to me. I discovered the same coaching techniques that worked for life coaching also worked for athletes and, ultimately, also worked for my staff. The principles were very much the same; however, the application was a little different. I began studying more sports psychology theories to help my coaching practice with athletes. The more I studied sports psychology, the more I found that those techniques continued to transfer into the world of business with ease. I had to know more! So, I enrolled in a psychology PhD program. The more I learned about psychology, the more I noticed distinctive similarities among the challenges each person I coached was facing. Business leaders, entrepreneurs, athletes, and people in their everyday lives suffered from many of the same afflictions: low motivation, self-doubt, a lack of proper goal-setting techniques, confidence issues, and a huge fear of failure. Many of them experienced occasional anxiety and depression. The symptoms, goals, and desired outcomes varied; however, the causes were pretty much the same. It all started and ended with their mindset. I realized that if I could help them change their mindsets, I could help them become unstoppable!

Each person I coached was in a different situation. Although they had different visions of success, the fundamental techniques that worked for an athlete attempting to improve her race times worked for an executive who wanted to improve his leadership skills, which also worked for anyone striving to improve their relationships and get more out of life. That's when it hit me: What if I combined what I knew about psychology, sports coaching, executive leadership coaching, and life coaching into one streamlined package that delivered the fastest, most potent results? I was onto something and, at that time, I knew it was big. However, I didn't know how big. It wasn't until after I had put together the high performance mindset shift tools and put them into action that I realized the incredible power every person has at their disposal. It doesn't take any special gear, supplements, or hours of therapy to unleash this ability. The techniques are explained in Part II, "Mindset Shift Tools." In those chapters, I'll teach you simple exercises you can do to train your mind and develop the high performance mindset you need to live your best life.

In **Chapter 6**, "Create New Positive Beliefs," I'll show you how to create beliefs that drive and reinforce your positive thoughts. Then, in **Chapter 7**, "The Kick-Ass You," I'll teach you why affirmations are the fastest and easiest way to ignite your confidence. Let's be honest, you might think you can buy confidence by surrounding yourself with whatever impresses other people; however, you can't just buy confidence at any store and you can't fake it either. Confidence comes from within, and you already have it. You merely need to uncover it by focusing on what you have instead of what you don't have. I'll show you how you can use affirmations to quickly send your confidence through the roof.

Another important element of developing a high performance mindset is thought management. Thought management is a mindset shift tool that teaches you how to stay in the moment. When you're in the moment, you're at your peak of high performance. Being in the moment isn't about focusing on what you're doing at this moment in time; in a way, it's about doing *without* thinking about your action. For example, a baseball player at bat doesn't want to think about hitting the ball movement by movement. The last thing he wants to think about is the mechanics of hitting that ball. Thinking through the motions requires sending information from the subconscious mind to the prefrontal cortex of your brain and then to the motor cortex, which takes more time and slows down your actions. In **Chapter 8**, "Own Your Focus," I'll show you how to stay in the moment.

One of the most powerful techniques that transfers from sports to business leadership to everyday life is visualization, also known as sports imagery. Do you want to know a secret? Your mind does not recognize the difference between reality and your imagination. You read that right. Your mind processes what you visualize in your mind and what happens in real life the same way. You might find that hard to believe. Think about a time when you woke up in the middle of the night in a panic after a nightmare. Your heart was racing, you were breathing erratically and you were covered in sweat. That is the result of your body responding to mental imagery. Research—through the utilization of functional magnetic resonance imaging, or *fMRI*—shows the *same* parts of a person's brain fire during visualization *and* when that person actually performs the task they're visualizing. Visualization is essentially mental practice for reality and a way for you to prepare your brain for what you want to make happen in your life. I'll teach you how you can use visualization to your advantage in **Chapter 9**, "Visualize Yourself to a High Performance Mindset."

The final chapters comprise Part III, "Putting It All Together." My greatest test in life has been raising a daughter. While it can be challenging for a single dad to raise a young lady, having a strong, independent, and loving mother helped me become a great dad. Some men think they're supposed to be warriors and not show any emotion because being emotional, for a man, is a sign of weakness. I thank Mom for teaching me that it is safe to experience emotions as a man. Her love and support empowered me to become a loving and supportive father to my own child. We're all emotional creatures and I'm grateful to my mom for teaching me that being an emotional man is healthy. Growing up that way made me stronger and more authentic, not weak and powerless. It also taught me the importance of love and relationships in developing the high performance mindset. We'll talk more about relationships in **Chapter 10**, "Relationships with Others and Yourself."

Raising my daughter, coaching athletes, executives, and people who want more out of life, having a great career, and working toward my PhD could have been the pinnacle of my success, and I do feel successful every single day. However, I continue to learn and seek opportunities to do more with my life. I get there by setting goals and achieving outcomes through process work and by improving my performance, which I'll discuss in detail in **Chapter 11**, "Crush Your Goals."

In **Chapter 12**, "Unlocking Your Purpose with the High Performance Mindset," you'll learn about your most important purpose in life and how you can fulfill that purpose every single day.

Finally, in **Chapter 13**, "The Finish Line," I'll hand over the keys to the high performance mindset so you can take the wheel and start seeing results right away.

As I mentioned previously, I've researched, tweaked, honed, tested, and personally applied every technique I'm going to teach you. When I was developing the mindset shift techniques, if something worked for one client and didn't work for other clients, I would tweak it until it did, or I threw it out. Every technique works *consistently*. I'm not going to waste your time with high performance mindset tools that only work sometimes, for some people.

Athletes and executives have experienced life-changing results in as little as one hour by using the techniques within this book through my coaching. One hour! Imagine what's possible using these techniques every day for the rest of your life.

While you're learning how to develop your high performance mindset, you'll also learn to see words differently. I'll teach you about the power of linguistics and about the words *thought*, *self-talk*, *focus*, *attention*, and *concentration*—and what those words actually mean. You'll find out why meditation and mindfulness aren't as mysterious as they sound. In fact, the backend of a high performance mindset constitutes the underlying reason that meditation and mindfulness practice work.

I hope you'll read this whole book and put into practice everything you learn. Reading is the first step; however, the magic—your transformation to the high performance mindset—only happens if you *apply* it. Action through application is a critical component of this book.

What you think, you manifest. Your thoughts create your reality. I'm giving you the tools to control your thoughts and think differently, to think effectively. Once you apply the mindset shift tools, you'll have the power to control your thoughts, change your reality, and own your destiny!

It is a shift, transforming from a low-performing mindset to a high-performing mindset. It's one of the most dramatic changes you can make in your life and it's closer than you could have imagined. It changed everything for me and it can change everything for you, too!

Let's get going!

PART I

YOUR MINDSET AND HOW TO CHANGE IT

CHAPTER

WHAT IS A HIGH PERFORMANCE MINDSET?

The high performance mindset. What does this mean? It might sound complex to you; however, it's not.

If you were to look up *high performance* in the dictionary, you'd find that it means *better, faster,* or *more efficient*. If you looked up the word *mindset*, you'd find that it means *mental attitude*. If we simply put *high performance* and *mindset* together, we get this: *a high performance mindset is a better, faster, and more efficient mental attitude.*

> *The high performance mindset **makes your best life possible.***

With a high performance mindset, you live your life in the driver's seat instead of the passenger seat. By choosing to create positive thoughts, you'll create fulfilling experiences, which create a happier, more fulfilled life. The sooner you begin, the faster you'll see results. You can start doing it today. Within these pages, I'll help you understand how your mind works, which will give you some clues about how it affects your life and why you have to learn to control your thoughts.

*The high performance mindset **allows you to have more positive thoughts, which lead to more fulfilling experiences** that make your best life possible.*

Here are some examples of how your mind affects your life: You've probably noticed that whenever you attempt to stay away from something, it keeps coming up in your life over and over again. Or that when one thing goes wrong during your day, everything else seems to go wrong as the day progresses. Those occurrences aren't coincidental; they're due to the fact that when you think about something, you direct your life toward it. Whatever captures your attention holds your focus and preoccupies your thoughts, pulling you—and your life—right along with it.

With a high performance mindset, you control what you focus on and think about. Focus on what you *want* in life instead of what you *don't* want. Learning how to control your thoughts is where most people get hung up. They don't think controlling their thoughts is possible. However, you *can* control your thoughts, your emotions, and your actions, and create a mindset that's driven by personal decision and accountability. Once you learn how to do that, you can create more positive thoughts that lead to fulfilling experiences.

Developing a high performance mindset requires more than thoughts, though; it also requires action. In life, *status quo* doesn't actually exist. Things are always moving. When you stop, the world doesn't stop with you. Time passes and things continue to happen. So, while you're sitting still, doing the same things, others around you are not. This means you're actually *regressing*. You need to act in order to progress; it's the only way. Again, developing a high performance mindset requires *ACTION*. How do you take action? By learning and then applying what you learn. As long as you continue to learn and take action, you're progressing. Once you act, you can evaluate the results of your actions, learn from those results, and act again—with consideration for what you learned from your results each time.

*The high performance mindset allows you to have more positive thoughts, **which promotes learning,*** *action, applying what you learn from your actions, and making progress with more fulfilling experiences that make your best life possible.*

Although this is all pretty straightforward so far, one *very* important piece is required for the high performance mindset to work. The most critical component is positive thinking. It's the main ingredient. You can't continue to learn and take action without a positive attitude. This isn't about viewing the world through rose-colored glasses, though. The world isn't perfect and there's plenty of negative stuff. However, you can train your mind to reframe the negatives in your life as positives. That way, instead of obstacles, the negatives become opportunities and challenges for learning and growing.

*The high performance mindset **employs a positive attitude** that allows you to have more positive thoughts, which promotes learning, action, applying what you learn from your actions, and making progress with more fulfilling experiences that make your best life possible.*

Do you know what the main cause of frustration, anger, let down, and disappointment is? Unmet expectations! These are the expectations we place on how other people should act or respond. However, *your* expectations are based on *your* view of the world, not other people's. Everyone has their own personal view of the world, based on their life experiences. So, it's not reasonable to expect people to see the world the same way you do—or to act or react to it the way you do. Letting go of your expectations frees you from the frustration, anger, let down, and disappointment caused by other people's actions. In fact, research shows that having lower expectations leads to a positive impact on your overall happiness. Lowering our expectations improves the likelihood that expectations get met leading to a boost in your happiness.[1] For example, if you go to a casino with three hundred dollars and you expect nothing but to have a good time, winning fifty dollars will increase your happiness because fifty dollars exceeded your expectations. However, if you go to the casino with three hundred dollars expecting to double your money and only win fifty dollars, your expectations are not met, thus negatively impacting your happiness. Which outcome would you choose? Right!

I can personally attest to this research. I am a genuinely happy person and I must credit my happiness mainly to lowering my expectations of others. Honestly, I'm never surprised by another person's actions. That may be hard for you to believe. It's true though: I'm not surprised by

---

1 Wolfram Schultz, ed., "A computational and neural model of momentary subjective well-being," Proceedings of the National Academy of Sciences of the United States of America, accessed May 23, 2017, at: http://www.pnas.org/content/111/33/12252.abstract

their actions because they're human. We like to think of people as robots; however, we're far from being robots, and as humans, our responses to stimuli aren't always consistent. There are obvious areas where expectations are necessary. For example, a director should have expectations for his employees that are based on the job description and a code of conduct. Expectations for work being performed per a contract are another area where we have something set by a contract. Outside of areas such as constructional labor or employment, limiting your expectations will improve your level of happiness.

Having a positive attitude would be easier if the world was devoid of negativity, but that's not the case. Negativity can come from many sources, and although you may not be able to control this negativity, you do have a choice in how you respond. It's not what happens to you; it's your response that shapes the trajectory of your future. You've heard the saying "Misery loves company." It's true. People can be a source of negativity, and negative people want you to be negative, too. You can give in to that negativity, or you can choose to respond to it with a positive attitude. For example, if someone at work is in a bad mood and they complain about the workload, everyone else is bound to join in and pile on more complaints. You can either add to the negativity or you can find something positive to say about the work, like, "I'm just thankful to have a job!" or comment on the fact that—with the current workload—we have job security for a long time!

You can also choose to respond positively to the negativity that arises from events and circumstances. For example, if you get a flat tire, that's not a good thing. Getting a flat tire is not what most people call fun, and your first reaction might be to respond negatively. You can either get mad, or you can choose to stay calm and collected and handle the situation as it is. Maybe getting a flat tire is an opportunity for you to learn how to change a flat tire or to call someone who can help. In the grand scheme of things, it's not a big deal. Maybe life is telling you to slow down and be more present. Anyway, you learn, take action, and observe your outcome. The results—a mended tire—are positive and you can enjoy your success. Instead of viewing the flat tire as something to get upset about, now you can think about the event as being granted the opportunity to learn how to change a tire. Our lives are built on both positive and negative experiences; how we choose to react to them is the difference between action and stagnation, progression and regression. It's the difference between learning, acting, and progress, and staying in a low-performing rut.

Finally, mastering a high performance mindset requires self-care and introspection. Self-care creates a framework of respect for yourself and for those around you and leads to growth and development at the highest levels. We'll talk about this more in upcoming chapters.

Once you've learned and practiced the methods in this book, they'll become habits. You'll do them naturally and with no conscious effort. You'll continue to grow your mindset and reap greater rewards—without even thinking about it. That's the magic of the high performance mindset. With practice, it becomes part of who you are.

CHAPTER

THE EVER-EVOLVING MIND

For a very long time, it was widely believed that the brain didn't change past a certain age. The belief was that you could only learn new things during a small window of time, and then you were done. Your brain stopped learning, changing, and growing. That turned out to be far from the truth and, in fact, your brain is capable of changing throughout your entire life. Your brain can be rewired with new pathways through learning. This is called *neuroplasticity*. Think of your brain as malleable plastic that you can form into the brain you want. Because of neuroplasticity, you can build new neural pathways that aren't good for you—like looking for the downside of every experience or dwelling on negative thoughts—or, you can choose to build positive neural pathways that improve and enrich your life.

In psychology, therapeutic modalities like cognitive behavioral therapy, or CBT, validate neuroplasticity and prove that you can change how you think. In the simplest terms, if you imagine sticking a pH stick into a pool to see what the water's like, that's kind of what CBT does with your mind. Professionals can inspect your thoughts and see how they work for you or against you, and then help you build new processes to help them work better. Mindfulness and meditation are also validators of neuroplasticity, used to develop a conscious awareness of being present and also to change the way you process information over time. Your brain is constantly evolving and it's up to you to mold it so it serves you and your best interests. We'll talk about this more a little later.

The ever-evolving brain—and mind—makes the high performance mindset possible. You can change your thinking and develop a high performance mindset, and if you already *have* a high performance mindset, you can improve it. You can *always* improve your current thought processes. While the concepts are simple, you'll need drive, determination, and a willingness to do the work to make it happen. You can use neuroplasticity to your advantage to create a better, faster, and more efficient mental attitude. You can shift your mindset into high gear.

THE EVER-EVOLVING MIND AND YOU

The ever-evolving mind allows you to create dramatic change in your life. The alternative is settling for the brain—the mindset—you have and all its baggage. You can let negative past experiences and outdated beliefs guide your thoughts. Those experiences and beliefs may not be good for you. They may be holding you back and even doing a lot of damage to your life. You can't change the past; however, you can change how you respond to it. You can change how your brain handles past experiences and how it handles what's happening in your life right now and in the future.

Remember this?

The high performance mindset employs a positive attitude that allows you to have more positive thoughts, which promotes learning, action, applying what you learn from your actions, and making progress with more fulfilling experiences that make your best life possible.

You can do this! Because your mind is constantly evolving, you can change your mind to develop a positive attitude and have more positive thoughts. You can open your mind to learning and take action. This will lead to progress and improve your experiences.

If you have a victim mentality or are always feeling sorry for yourself, that mentality keeps you from achieving your goals. It can be debilitating and may limit your potential for reaching sports goals on the field, business goals in the office, and personal life goals. You can learn how to change that mentality. You can meet and exceed your personal and professional goals, and you can also have the kinds of relationships you want and deserve. Two excellent examples of people who overcame their past experiences and went on to achieve phenomenal success are Les Brown and Oprah Winfrey. Les, the best-selling author of *Live Your Dreams*, was once homeless. He's now a multimillionaire. Oprah was abused as a child and she was able to change the way she thinks and apply positivity and optimism to her life. Look where she is now. Who doesn't know who Oprah is and what an inspiration she is to everyone around her? Situations do not define you unless you succumb to them.

Thanks to your ever-evolving brain, you can even change your deepest beliefs. With a high performance mindset, you're always learning and evolving. Your beliefs will change as you continue to learn and apply the lessons you've gained through the process. You can begin to see the world through a different lens and in a more positive light, and that can change your deepest beliefs about yourself, other people, and life.

Don't be put off by the need for constant learning. Remember, I didn't like high school and I barely graduated. However, I realized that learning is necessary to grow, so I found ways to obtain knowledge that worked for me. Even though I used to dislike reading, I now read all the time, because it's a great way to learn. If you don't like to read, you can listen to audiobooks and watch online tutorials. Find any way to learn that you enjoy—just learn, and then apply what you learned in your career, your sport, or in your life.

People with a high performance mindset are always learning. They see obstacles as opportunities for growing and learning something new. As you learn, your brain changes, making new pathways to more positive thoughts that lead to more fulfilling experiences. Those experiences will motivate you to learn more. Your fulfilling experiences are your new life. These experiences might include finishing or even winning a race. They could involve getting a raise, a promotion, or it could be a better relationship with your kids or your spouse. Whatever you want to improve in your life is possible when you change your thoughts, and you *can* change your thoughts. I'm going to show you how.

Change is scary, right? And changing your brain—that's just crazy! Don't be afraid. This kind of change is good and it's not crazy at all. In fact, it's required. Change is happening all around us. Your body, your mind—the weather. Everything is changing, and we have to get on board with change in order to have a high performance mindset. Honestly, change is required to learn the truth about yourself and the world. Did you know that children who live far from the ocean are more likely to be afraid of water than kids who live near the sea? Why is that? The ocean isn't more dangerous for one group of children than it is for the other. The difference is that kids who grew up near the ocean are used to it. They've seen it and aren't afraid. The kids who grew up inland don't know what to expect from the ocean. They've never seen water much deeper than their bathtub and all that bottomless water scares them to death. We all grow up with fears of the unknown. However, just because we're unfamiliar with something doesn't mean that thing is necessarily dangerous. Many of the fears—and beliefs—we develop as children aren't rational; however, we often hang onto them into adulthood.

I once coached a client who was afraid of flying. I asked her "What do you know about flying in an airplane?" Her response was nothing more than "It's not safe!" I assigned her some homework: Research flying. The next week, we met again and I asked her what she'd learned about flying. She said she'd learned that flying is one of the safest forms of transportation—that it's much safer than driving a car, and the odds of dying in a crash are much, much lower in a plane than in a car. This knowledge helped ease her fear of flying. For many people, fear stems from a lack of knowledge and the idea that our beliefs are factual. You can punch fear in the face by learning more about that which you fear.

That's an example of how learning can change your beliefs and your attitude. Learning can turn something you fear into something you look forward to, like going for a swim in the ocean or getting on a plane to visit your grandmother.

The ever-evolving mind allows you to educate yourself, learn, and grow. It allows you to change your mindset.

CHAPTER

UNDERSTANDING YOUR MINDSET

Teachers, scientists, and world leaders have sought to describe people's thoughts, their connection to existence, and their influence in people's lives. Some of them have made some pretty powerful statements.

"I think, therefore I am," came from the seventeenth-century French philosopher René Descartes.

Indian activist Mahatma Gandhi said, "Your beliefs become your thoughts. Your thoughts become your words. Your words become your actions. Your actions become your habits. Your habits become your values. Your values become your destiny."

The concept of thoughts being rooted in beliefs and those thoughts driving your destiny weren't invented yesterday; this concept has been around for a long time in philosophy. How you can use it to your advantage isn't so obvious, though. A lot of the research is buried in textbooks and scientific journals that most people will never read.

Simply put, your mindset has two parts. You have a conscious mind, which consists of all the thoughts you're aware of, and you have a subconscious mind, which is everything else that's going on in your head below your state of consciousness. Although you aren't aware of your subconscious mind, both parts of your mindset affect your actions.

YOUR CONSCIOUS MIND

Thoughts only occur in your conscious mind. Research from various laboratories indicates that you have as many as 70,000 conscious thoughts per day. The Cleveland Clinic puts the average number of thoughts per day at 60,000 and found that 95 percent of your thoughts are repetitive and 80 percent of your thoughts are negative.[2] Due to the subjective nature of thoughts, a reliable calculation of daily thoughts is pretty challenging, so—for

---

2   "Don't Believe Everything You Think," Cleveland Clinic Wellness, accessed May 5, 2017, at: http://www.clevelandclinicwellness.com/programs/NewSFN/pages/default. aspx?Lesson=3&Topic=2&UserId=00000000-0000-0000-0000-000000000705

the sake of this book—we'll stick to the lower end and say you have between 12,000 and 50,000 thoughts per day, which means that you can have as many as 40,000 negative thoughts and 38,000 of them are repeated—every day. Whew, that's a lot of thinking!

Think about that for a moment. Most of the thousands of thoughts you have every day are negative, and you repeat them to yourself over and over again. Since thoughts drive learning, action, progress, and experiences, it's no wonder that many people struggle with low self-confidence and motivation. The good news is that you can replace your negative thoughts with positive ones. You can develop a more positive attitude and create more positive thoughts, which in turn manifest a better reality.

If your car was low on gas and there was a gas station nearby with cheap gas because the gas had water in it, would you fill your tank with that watered-down gas? Of course not. Even though it might save you some money, it's going to cause engine problems. By the same token, if you fill your head with the most convenient thoughts—which are usually negative—your head is going to develop all kinds of knocks and pings. You don't want a noisy engine—you want a mindset that purrs like a kitten when you're at rest and roars like a lion when you hit the gas.

You need good gas to do that. You need to fill up with positive thoughts.

Here's one last thought before we move on to Part III—if you ruin your car with cheap gas, you can trade it in. You only get one brain. Take care of it. Keep it clean. It will serve you well and take you wherever you want to go. That's the cool thing about the high performance mindset.

THE POWER—AND THE CONFUSION—OF LINGUISTICS ON YOUR CONSCIOUS MIND

Linguistics refers to language, and *your* linguistics—the words you use in your head and speak out loud—are your thoughts. Due to the power of linguistics, it's essential for you to understand the meaning of the words you use. When you verbalize those words by saying them out loud, they become even more real to you and your conscious mind.

This leads me to one of the most important areas of this book that I want you to really take in. Linguistics has a powerful effect on your mindset, and it can cause a lot of confusion, too. For example, let's talk about the vocabulary people often use.

REAL-LIFE POWER OF LINGUISTICS

An unfortunate, personal event made me aware of the power of linguistics. I was at work one day and my mother called me. She was crying, and that wasn't normal for my mom. I asked her, "What's going on?" and she said, "I have something I need to tell you, Craig. I just left the doctor and I have breast cancer. I wanted to make sure that you knew."

I remember the pause. I then asked my mother, "Is this fixable, Mom?" and she said, "The doctor thinks so." I was very matter-of-fact about the issue, and I said, "So, we know where the finish line is. This is basically a marathon. We know where we are. We know where the finish line is. We just have to get there together." She agreed.

Then we talked for a few more minutes. I told her I loved her, said, "We'll figure this out," and I hung up the phone. I sat there in my chair for about ten minutes, numb. I couldn't process this new information while I was speaking to my mom on the phone, and I couldn't process it sitting there, either.

I finally got up and told one of the women in my office that I'd gotten a call from my mom. "My mom has cancer," I said. As soon as the words came out of my mouth, I fell apart. I just cried and I cried, and I had to get out of there. I told her I had to leave. I picked up my keys and left, and I didn't come back for the rest of the day. In reflection of that time, I realized the power of the words we speak and how important it is to know their meaning, because they affect us in more ways than we ever would have thought. You can read about her story at craigwillard.com/blog/mymomsblessing.

EXERCISE 1: LINGUISTICS

Have you ever thought much about the words "thoughts," "focus," "self-talk," "concentration," and "attention?" I noticed that when I coached clients, many of them seemed very confused about the meanings of these words.

STEP ONE

For this exercise, in as few words as possible and without looking them up, write down your definitions of the following words.

1. Thoughts:
2. Focus:
3. Self-talk:
4. Concentration:
5. Attention:

What did you find out? Are they all different? Or do some of these words seem similar? This is something I have come to learn a lot about during my coaching—people do not always understand the words they use and what they actually mean or how they affect their mindset. One of the first things I do with my clients is teach the power of linguistics and more specifically, the five words you just defined in your own words.

Before moving forward, I want to share some raw data regarding this exercise. I surveyed people to find out what they thought these words meant for this book. One person told me that "thoughts" were what you were thinking about, while "focus" meant to dedicate all your thoughts to a single goal or subject. He believed that "self-talk" had to do with doubts, that when your mind found something interesting it got your "attention," and that "concentration" happened when your mind was consumed by something. Each person gave me slightly different answers, with one thing in common: They all believed there were major differences between thoughts, focus, self-talk, concentration, and attention. Is that what you found out? This survey exposed a major problem with teaching people about mindset. There's a lot of confusion around linguistics!

What if I told you that thoughts, focus, self-talk, concentration, and attention are the exact same thing when it comes to our mindset?

That's right! Thoughts, focus, self-talk, concentration, and attention are the same. Think about it this way: When you have a thought, you have to talk to yourself about it. That is your self-talk. Your self-talk is what you focus on. When you focus on something, you concentrate on it, and you give all your attention to it. So essentially, thoughts, focus, self-talk, concentration, and attention are the same things. Make sense? Good.

STEP TWO

To prove this to yourself, think about a red ball. Close your eyes and imagine that red ball. Then open your eyes and keep reading.

Did you think about a red ball? Yes, your thought was "red ball." Were you focused on that red ball? Yes, you focused on the red ball. Did you say the words "red ball" in your head? Yes, "red ball" was your self-talk. Self-talk is what you say to yourself inside your head. You can't say one thing to yourself while you think about something else. They're always the same. Was your attention on the red ball? How about your concentration? Red ball, red ball, right? Don't be confused by different definitions of those words. Thoughts, focus, self-talk, concentration, and attention all mean the same thing.

★ ★ ★

Now that you know thought, self-talk, focus, concentration, and attention mean the same thing, I'll tell you why they're important. You own them. They're yours. You own your thoughts, your focus, your self-talk, your concentration, and your attention. You have a choice in what you think about, and your choices determine your actions and become your destiny.

It turns out that Gandhi fellow knew what he was talking about.

REAL-LIFE CONFUSION OF LINGUISTICS

Linguistics confusion can hinder our understanding of mindset, and it can cause misunderstandings in everyday life. You know that communication is critical to all aspects of life; however, I would suggest that how we communicate through linguistics and knowing what we are really saying is even more critical. The confusion over the words we use is very apparent when you think about it. What does "love" mean? Could you define it without using the word "love?" Many will say, "What do you mean? Love is love!" For another example, let's talk about the word "focus." I was at my daughter's softball practice one day. Her team, a bunch of eight-year-old girls, was in the outfield and their coach was on second base. He started hitting balls to them.

When they didn't attempt to catch the balls, the coach got upset and started yelling. "You have to focus, and you're not focusing!" He hit a few more balls. Nothing changed. After practice, we got her things together and started walking to the truck as we normally do. I helped her with her cleats, put her in the truck, and we began to head home. As a mental coach, I knew when the softball coach asked the girls to focus, they wouldn't change a thing. Eight-year-olds aren't taught things like this; however, as adults, we expect them to know—even when we, as adults, may not truly understand what "focus" means.

"Hey, I noticed when the coach told you all to focus, nothing happened. You all didn't do anything different," I said to my daughter as we drove home. She nodded in agreement. Nothing changed with their actions.

"Just curious, do you know what the word 'focus' means?"

"Nope," she said. "No clue."

She didn't know what it meant, and I'm willing to bet that if I asked her coach, he didn't know either. Chances are that someone yelled "focus" at him one time when he wasn't paying attention, and so he was just repeating it. This isn't uncommon and definitely isn't out of the norm.

That's the problem with using words that people don't understand or even expecting them to understand without clarity. Nothing changes!

A LOOK AT MULTITASKING

Your mind stays busy focusing, concentrating, and giving all its attention to those 12,000 to 50,000 thoughts every day. That's a lot of thoughts to squeeze into just one day. So, what about multitasking? Can you multitask?

EXERCISE 2: TAKE THE MULTITASKING TEST

As a high performance coach, this is a question I ask every one of my clients: "Can you multitask?" Most of them quickly reply with "Absolutely!" to which I respond, "Great, let's give it a test." Follow along with me here and you can test yourself.

STEP ONE

Without speaking out loud, use your self-talk to count from one to ten in your head:

1, 2, 3, 4, 5, 6, 7, 8, 9, 10.

STEP TWO

OK, great. Now do it again three times in a row, as fast as you can:

1, 2, 3, 4, 5, 6, 7, 8, 9, 10, 1, 2, 3, 4, 5, 6, 7, 8, 9, 10, 1, 2, 3, 4, 5, 6, 7, 8, 9, 10.

Did you do it? Nice!

STEP THREE

Now, out loud, I want you to sing or speak "If you're happy and you know it clap your hands."

If you're happy and you know it, clap your hands.

STEP FOUR

Good job. Now say or sing it again three times in a row, back to back.

If you're happy and you know it, clap your hands.

If you're happy and you know it, clap your hands.

If you're happy and you know it, clap your hands.

Good job!

Next, what I want you to do is—in your head—count as fast as you can from one to ten three times *while at the same time* saying "If you're happy and you know it, clap your hands" out loud three times.

How did you do? Did you laugh? You couldn't do it, could you?

★ ★ ★

So, here's the truth. If I chase two rabbits, I get neither. At the conscious level, multitasking isn't possible. You validated this in Exercise 2. You can only think about one thing at a time. It is one thought or another—never both simultaneously. Some people think they can truly multitask; however, what they are doing is switching their attention back and forth real fast. This is very inefficient.

To illustrate this further, think about a time when you did something that required your total concentration. For example, have you ever put together a piece of IKEA furniture? It can be a bit painful—so many pieces and parts! You lay out the instructions and the parts. You have your tools ready, and as you begin to build that piece of furniture, your friend walks in and starts talking to you about his love life. He's spilling his guts to you about his girl while you're looking at the instructions and putting this thing together. Confusion sets in. You notice that you're not able to read the instructions, put the furniture together, and listen to what your friend is saying. Ultimately, you end up asking your friend to give you some time to put the furniture together and then you can give him your full attention. Or, you give up on the IKEA furniture for now and just listen to what your friend has to say.

REAL-LIFE MULTITASKING MISTAKES

Sometimes, our lack of ability to consciously multitask can get us into trouble. For example, people often attempt to multitask when they have conversations. Instead of actively listening to what the other person is saying, they spend their energy thinking about how they're going to respond *while the other person is talking*. If they formulate a good response in their head, they don't want to lose that thought so they focus on it—instead of the other person's words. This disconnects people. Being engaged and actively listening to the other person will improve your communication skills. As Stephen Covey said, "Seek first to understand, then to be understood."[3]

You can't listen to a person and think about your response at the same time. If you challenge this, you miss their half of the conversation. Then you're not even having a conversation with another person, you're just talking.

My mother used to say, "God gave us two ears and one mouth. We should listen twice as much as we talk." As it turns out, Mom was right. If you care enough about the person, listen to them with intention and then respond after you have finished listening; this can limit arguments and misunderstandings a great deal.

---

3   Stephen R. Covey, *The 7 Habits of Highly Effective People: Powerful Lessons in Personal Change, Anniversary Edition* (New York: Simon & Schuster, 2013), page 249.

Okay, I know what you're thinking. Sure, there's one way you *can* multitask—just one, though. If you've done something so many times that it's automatic, you can do it while you're thinking about something else. For example, you can sweep the floor and talk on the phone at the same time. You've swept the floor so many times that it's automatic for you and you don't have to think about it when you're doing it. Building a piece of IKEA furniture isn't automatic, because you haven't built that particular piece of furniture enough times to do it automatically. If you teach someone to paint a room for the first time, they would have to pay attention to the task at hand and wouldn't be able to hold much of a conversation at the same time. That's the multitasking caveat—it's only possible when one action is so automatic that it doesn't require your concentration.

YOUR SUBCONSCIOUS MIND

While your conscious thoughts occur in the conscious part of your mind, remember, your mindset has another part, and it's responsible for storing a lot of information you use to make decisions.

Your conscious mind accounts for a mere 2 percent of your thinking power. The other 98 percent is your subconscious mind.[4] If your conscious mind processes all the thoughts that you're aware of, then what goes on in your subconscious mind?

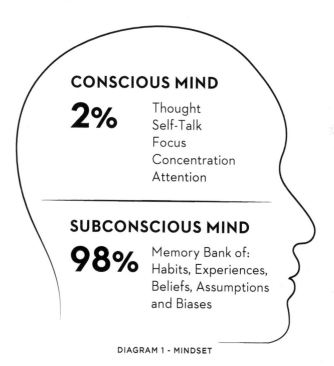

CONSCIOUS MIND

2% Thought
Self-Talk
Focus
Concentration
Attention

SUBCONSCIOUS MIND

98% Memory Bank of:
Habits, Experiences,
Beliefs, Assumptions
and Biases

DIAGRAM 1 - MINDSET

Take a look at Diagram 1. Your subconscious mind is essentially a memory bank for your habits, experiences, assumptions, biases, and repressed memories. It has been said that some of them are there because they are too disturbing to allow the conscious mind to become aware of. Information is being stored in your subconscious mind

---

4   Michael S. Gazzaniga, "Principles of Human Brain Organization Derived from Split-Brain Studies," *Neuron, Vol. 14, 217-228*, February, 1995, accessed May 14, 2017, at: www.cell.com/neuron/abstract/0896-6273(95)90280-5

throughout your lifetime. What does it do with this information? I like to think of the conscious mind as sitting at a podium on a stage, asking the audience—the subconscious mind—what it knows about a particular thought.

When your conscious mind has an experience, it asks your subconscious mind "What do you know about this?" Then, your subconscious mind draws upon everything *it* knows about the experience to help your conscious mind understand it quickly. Your subconscious mind might have previous experience and valuable information about whatever it is you're seeing, hearing, smelling, tasting, feeling, or thinking. It pulls information quickly, because it is always looking to protect you. It tells your conscious mind everything it knows about that thing, good or bad. However, your subconscious mind likes to generalize that information to make it quicker to access and easier for your conscious mind to understand its present experience. Your subconscious mind enjoys looking for similarities and patterns between your current and past experiences. Doing this takes less time and burns less energy than thoroughly analyzing each new experience. It's more efficient for your mindset to operate this way. You can make faster judgments, form faster opinions, and have faster reaction times.

You might see a cloud in the sky and think "Hey, that looks

like the state of Kentucky" because you live in Kentucky, and you are familiar with its shape. If you're not from the state of Kentucky, then your subconscious mind won't tell you the cloud looks like anything other than a cloud. It might tell you the cloud looks like something else that's stored in your memory bank though. Your subconscious mind might recall a similarity between the present and the past, and you get a feeling called *déjà vu*, which is French for "already seen." When you experience *déjà vu*, you might feel like you're reliving a past experience. That ability can protect you, especially if you're in a dangerous situation and your subconscious mind provides information that allows your conscious mind to make a quick decision, like getting out of the way of a speeding car or stepping back from the edge of a cliff.

However, you can't always trust it to provide your conscious mind with the information you need to make good decisions. Your subconscious mind can feed your conscious mind information that's false because, remember, it's made up of all those habits, experiences, assumptions, biases, and beliefs you've developed in your lifetime, yet in a generalized way. If your subconscious mind is so unreliable, and it's your mindset's first source for sorting out new experiences, how do you know if what you're thinking about those experiences is true or false?

Here's another funny thing about your subconscious mind: Everything in your memory bank is true *to you*. This is why everything stored there comprises your beliefs. If it wasn't your truth, it wouldn't be your belief.

Finally, as I mentioned earlier, your subconscious mind can't tell the difference between what's real and what you visualize. You can visualize anything and your subconscious mind believes it. That should give you a clue as to why visualization is so important to developing the high performance mindset. We will talk about this in more detail in Chapter 9.

HOW YOUR SUBCONSCIOUS MIND AFFECTS YOUR RELATIONSHIPS

Your subconscious mind affects your conscious mind, and it also affects your relationships. As a child, you interacted with your parents, grandparents, or other caregivers and formed relationships with them. You also observed how those people formed relationships with each other. You were then imprinted with how those relationships worked and—because your subconscious mind loves patterns and similarities—you usually end up duplicating them. On a subconscious level, your mind is always encouraging you to repeat your experiences in relationships. Have you ever told your spouse, "You're just like my mom!" or "You're just like my dad!" This is why!

Your subconscious mind acts like a rip current, too, pulling you away from new experiences. If it doesn't recognize an experience, it can encourage you to not have that experience; or, if it recognizes an experience you had before that didn't end well for you, it can warn you away from that experience. This is how it protects you, and this is also how it can force you to repeat—over and over again—experiences that may be bad for you, even though you don't know they are. It wants you to do nothing more than survive. This conflicts with your desire to thrive.

Seriously. Your subconscious mind can hurt you, for example, by encouraging you to mimic a relationship you were in, or that you witnessed—such as the one between your caregivers—that was problematic. Your subconscious mind likes for you to recreate bad relationships from your childhood that hurt you in an attempt to fix the pain associated with them, and that's just not possible. Unfortunately, unless you recognize what your subconscious mind is doing, you may keep repeating that problematic relationship over and over again in your own life. You're unable to fix the past, and you most likely won't be able to make the current relationship right either.

That's why being a present and active parent or caregiver is so important to your children's future. If you're an absent parent, your children may grow up to seek out absent partners, believing they can control them and make them remain present in an attempt to repair their own emotional damage. Subconsciously, they want to fix that past relationship. You can imagine how that usually works out. An absent parent may also drive the child to feel as if they are not worthy of love and so they self-sabotage relationships, especially those they feel they are not worthy of.

Once you recognize the pattern, you can do something about it. Your subconscious mind may be telling you to find a partner who's absent; however, you can decide to focus on what you do want instead of what you don't want. You can focus on finding a partner who's present.

AVOIDANCE CREATES ATTRACTION

There's a good reason to focus on what you *want*, instead of what you *don't* want. When you attempt to avoid something, you attract it—in mass quantities.

You may have heard a friend say, "I don't know what I want; however, I know what I don't want." Oddly enough, that same friend keeps getting more of what they don't want. They end up in the same bad relationships, or in jobs they hate. Why is that?

It's because your subconscious mind doesn't understand negatives. It doesn't understand what you don't want. Your mind only understands what you're focused on, whether or not these thoughts are about something you *want* or *don't want*. So, if you tell yourself "I'm not going to date assholes," you're probably going to end up dating assholes. If you say to yourself, "I'm not going to be late for work," you'll probably be late. And if you say, "I'm not going to skip the gym," you will almost certainly not make it to the gym. While you might think, "I'm not going to skip the gym" sounds positive, it actually isn't because, without some self-doubt about going, you wouldn't have to say this to yourself.

Your mind doesn't understand the "not" part of the equation, so you have to train yourself to focus on what you want, instead of dwelling on what you don't want. Take, for example, your friend who seems to always find himself in bad jobs or relationships. Rather than focusing on what he doesn't want, he should figure out what he wants in a new career or a relationship and focus on that, instead. Likewise, if you start every day expecting to face challenges that will make you angry, tell yourself "I am going to find the silver lining in all situations." Use your self-talk to focus on what you want to happen: "I will be on time for work today, and I'm excited about going to the gym." Statements like this are much more beneficial subconsciously.

YOUR SUBCONSCIOUS MIND PREPARES YOU FOR THE WORST

Your subconscious mind looks out for you, sometimes by preparing you for the worst. If your conscious mind asks it for information about something, your subconscious mind searches its memory bank of past experiences for something similar. When it does this, it may zero in on something bad so you can prepare and protect yourself. For example, if you walk through a tunnel and see something coiled up in the dark, your subconscious mind is more likely to tell you it's a snake than a rope. Although your conscious mind will kick in and figure out that it's a rope, your first thought is "snake."

This response by your subconscious mind can protect you from dangerous situations. It can also cause you a lot of grief. For example, if you text your girlfriend and she doesn't respond right away, you might begin to freak out thinking she's with another guy because the last time this happened to you, your then-girlfriend didn't respond because she actually *was* with another guy. That's how your subconscious mind can get you into trouble. Then, when you finally get ahold of her, you lash out and question why she didn't answer only to discover that she was at the movies with her girlfriend the whole time, and her phone was in silent mode.

By now, you should have a good understanding of how the subconscious mind can help you—or hurt you. You can probably see why you'd want to manage that memory bank and make sure it's filled with valuable information that benefits you. I'll tell you how to do this soon.

HOW THE CONSCIOUS AND SUBCONSCIOUS MIND INTERACT

As I highlighted in Diagram 1, your conscious mind makes up about 2 percent of your thinking power. Now, let's explore that 2 percent in Diagram 2. The conscious mind interacts with the subconscious mind all the time. The conscious mind is always thinking. The mind doesn't shut off, nor does it have moments where it thinks about "nothing" as you may commonly hear. You may have heard someone say you need to "quiet your mind" or "calm your thinking." Both statements are really referring to control. However, do you know how to control your thinking? You will by the time you finish this book.

The point I'm making here is that either you control your conscious mind or it controls you. That's the overall decision you must make. As Diagram 2 shows, thoughts only come in two forms: They are either positive or they are negative. This is represented by two of the three arrows to the right of the head. The effects of a positive thought include happiness, success, gratitude, kindness, love, and affection. However, if your thought is negative, then you might experience worry, stress, anxiety, depression, anger, sweaty palms, and even nervousness, to name a few. With a high performance mindset, you take control of your thoughts and decide whether each one is positive or negative.

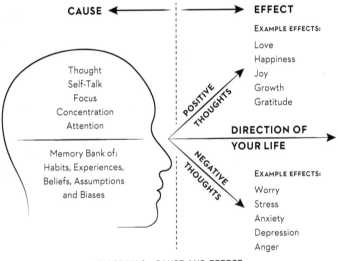

DIAGRAM 2 - CAUSE AND EFFECT

Again, every thought will be positive or negative depending on how you decide to perceive it. This diagram is a key element to understanding your mindset. On the left of the dotted line is what I call "cause." On the right side of the dotted line is the "effect." I say this because our thoughts create results, a.k.a. effects. Just knowing the effects of a positive versus a negative thought should be enough to motivate you to take control of your thoughts. Who wants to worry when they could be happy? You have the power to choose whether a thought is positive or negative. However, there's much more to it.

Beyond the emotional and physiological effects, *your life takes the direction of whichever you choose most often.* The middle arrow in Diagram 2 is your life's direction, and if you have more positive thoughts than negative thoughts, your life will go in a positive direction; you will attract more positive people and situations. Again, what you think, you manifest. If you have more negative thoughts than positive thoughts—well, you know where that leads you.

Your life becomes what you think and, like Gandhi tells us, your beliefs ultimately become your destiny—beliefs start with your thought/focus/self-talk.

Your positive and negative thoughts drive the direction of your life, and they attract similar people, circumstances, and events. Good attracts good, while bad attracts bad. You've probably heard of karma and even used it to explain something that happened to someone else. Bad karma

REAL-LIFE EFFECTS OF MEDICATING YOUR THOUGHTS

In the introduction, I pointed out that I was once diagnosed with general anxiety disorder and was put on medication to treat it. That medication made me feel like I was experiencing the world through a dull filter because, in a sense, I was. You see, when you go to a physician to express concerns over your anxiety and/or depression, they ask you what your symptoms are. For example, if you have a headache, you experience pain. However, just because you take medication to relieve the pain so you no longer feel the headache, the cause of that pain—the nerve pinch, or whatever is causing your headache—is still there. In both situations, physicians are accustomed to treating effects, a.k.a. symptoms. Thus, if you ever quit taking the medicine, what happens? That's right—the effects come back. Why? Medication doesn't treat causes which—in the case of anxiety—are the thoughts in your head and how you perceive them.

When I stopped taking that medication, all the *effects* came back and I knew that if I wanted to make them go away for good, I had to treat the *cause*. I had to take control of my thoughts and learn to focus on what I wanted in life instead of what I didn't want, and I had to learn how to turn more thoughts into positive ones.

The pills masked the real problems, which were my thinking and, as you recall, your thoughts are your self-talk, your focus, your concentration, and your attention. I worked very hard and as I improved my mindset, my issues subsided without medication. I had heard that I needed to control my thinking, I just didn't know how. When I realized my thinking was my self-talk, everything changed. I could change my self-talk, thus correcting the cause of my anxiety. By treating the cause, the effects disappeared on their own. I honestly have not suffered from anxiety in many years as a result. I'll provide you with the same tools that worked for me and all my clients as well, a little later.

In summary, the dotted, vertical line in the diagram separates the stimuli (cause) and the response (effect). The stimuli are our thoughts. The response is the positive and the negative effects of our thoughts and our emotional and physiological responses which influence our actions and the direction of our life. The key here is that treatments—such as pills for anxiety and depression—mask what's on the right, the effect. In order to truly resolve those effects, we have to deal with what's on the left, *the way we think*. Anxiety and depression are both thinking errors. They are things that we can absolutely overcome. This is how I've gotten away from general anxiety disorder. I haven't experienced anxiety in many, many years; I have learned that this is the true cause and I have worked really, really hard to correct it.

isn't a mystical power that curses people who do bad things. People who decide their thoughts are going to be negative attract negativity and their lives go in a direction that brings them bad things. Bad karma is nothing more than receiving negative results from negative thinking. Good karma works the same way. If you choose to see the world in a positive light and accept each thought as positive, your life will go in a positive direction. You'll attract positive people and experiences. Like attracts like.

If your friend did something bad to you, you might have thought, "Karma's going to get them eventually." Then, something bad happened to them or they did something that caused them to get hurt. You automatically pointed out this self-fulfilling prophecy, saying, "Hey, that's karma. You had it coming to you and you got it." In reality, your friend created his own negative karma with his negative thoughts. Again, it's not mystical. It's just how we think. Karma happens because what we focus on, we create. When you focus on something negative, things are going to come back to you in a negative manner. That includes wishing bad karma on someone else; so, if you wish bad karma on someone, that negative thinking will ultimately hurt you. Think twice before you wish bad karma on anyone—even if you feel they deserve it.

Remember, what you focus on, you create, and your

conscious thoughts—driven by your subconscious habits, experiences, assumptions, biases, and beliefs—will ultimately become your destiny.

YOUR MINDSET IN ACTION

As mentioned previously, every conscious thought you have is influenced by your subconscious mind.

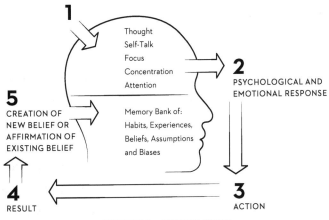

DIAGRAM 3 - MINDSET WHEEL

In Diagram 3, "Mindset Wheel," you can see how the conscious mind experiences life through the lens of the subconscious mind. Your view of the world is dramatically affected by your memory bank of biases and beliefs, which evolved from past experiences. The Mindset Wheel is the process that takes place when storing information within your subconscious mind.

When you experience a thought (1), your subconscious mind gives your conscious mind information about it based on past experiences. That information will make your conscious mind see the thought as positive or negative, which leads to an emotional and a physiological response (2). If your mind decides a thought is positive, you'll experience positive emotions and positive physiological responses. For example, you experience a positive thought and your response is to hold your head up in confidence, straighten your posture, turn your body toward someone, make eye contact, and smile. If your mind decides a thought is negative, you'll experience negative emotions and negative physiological responses. It may come in the form of a frown or a grimace, or you might experience physical pain, get sweaty palms, or display aggression. Your facial expression and body language change, and you tend to turn away from others and look down. This only causes more negative responses, because when you close yourself off to the world by turning away from people or consistently look down, you can't see the opportunities in front of you. Those who are happy don't display negative emotions or physiological responses, and vice versa. By paying attention to non-verbal cues, you can quickly recognize the state someone is in.

Your emotional and physiological responses to thoughts influence your actions (3). If you feel good, you smile and someone smiles back. If you feel bad, you scowl or frown and the person turns away. Positive thoughts cause you to open yourself up to opportunities, learn something new, or connect with someone. Negative thoughts cause you to shut down, neglect to act, and regress.

How you act produces a result (4). That result alone is not a success or a failure; you make a choice as to how you define your results. We'll talk more about failure in Chapter 7. From here, the result loops back into your mind through your sensory system, which is your vision, hearing, taste, smell, touch, and balance—however the result is realized (5).

This spinning of the Mindset Wheel is where our subconscious mind is programmed.

The good thing is, because of neuroplasticity, this wheel is capable of overwriting our subconscious mind with new information because our subconscious mind is constantly recording. It is always recording whatever we're saying and thinking. All of that stuff comes back around through our sensory system and is recorded as new beliefs, assumptions, and biases, or it affirms an existing belief.

This is important when you consider how the two parts of your mindset—the 2 percent conscious mind and the 98 percent subconscious mind shown in Diagram 2, "Cause and Effect"—interact. Your conscious mind is always taking in new information, and your subconscious mind is always telling it how to interpret that information. With a low performing mindset, you're at the mercy of your subconscious mind providing outdated information that wants to protect you from doing pretty much anything. As hard as it may be to believe, your mind only wants you to survive. It doesn't care whether you thrive. That's where the high performance mindset makes the largest difference. With a high performance mindset, you control how you perceive a thought, so you also control the emotional and physiological responses and your actions. You control how you gauge the results, and you can use that power to reinforce a positive belief or change a negative one.

THE NEGATIVE MINDSET VERSUS THE HIGH PERFORMANCE MINDSET

The most important factor in this equation is your power to be in control. The stimuli coming into your mind will receive a response from you. How you process the stimuli and respond to it is up to you.

The negative mindset decides that more thoughts are negative than positive. It receives stimuli, has a thought based upon the information offered by the subconscious mind and decides the thought is negative. The negative thought causes a negative physiological and emotional response. This leads to negative actions, a poor result, and ultimately being recorded as truth in your subconscious mind. People with a negative mindset suffer the consequences of their own personal choices. Even if you feel you are at the mercy of others, you still have a right to choose and a decision to make.

On the other hand, the high performance mindset decides that more thoughts are positive. People with a high performance mindset reap the benefits of their choices. When you have a high performance mindset, there's no difference between an obstacle and an opportunity, because they're the same thing, and they're positive. You can train your mind to accept every obstacle and every barrier as a challenge; or, you can train your mind to accept every obstacle as an opportunity to learn, act, progress, and create fulfilling experiences that lead to a happy life.

04
CHAPTER

TIME AND THE MIND: DEPRESSION, ANXIETY, AND HAPPINESS

In Chapter 3, we learned that our mindset contains two parts—the conscious and the subconscious. We learned what each part does, how they work together, and how we create habits. Now, I would like to bring your attention to another very important concept that ultimately affects your overall mindset, and thus controls your life. It's called *TIME* and it's critical to really understand this section in order to fire up your high performance mindset.

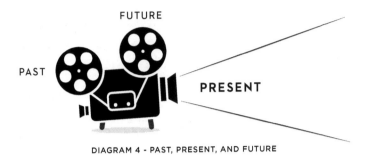

FUTURE

PAST

PRESENT

DIAGRAM 4 - PAST, PRESENT, AND FUTURE

When talking about time, one of the most critical concepts to understand is how our mind processes time. There are three points of time our mind understands. They are *future*, *past* and *present*. To help you with this concept, check out Diagram 4, "Past, Present, and Future." The old film projector has a front reel—the future—which indicates what hasn't happened yet. The rear reel is the past—what has already happened. Then, there is the projector light; this is the present. For example, if you're about to watch a movie, you will place the movie on the front reel. The movie itself is in the future because you have yet to see it. When that movie starts to play, the film slides down in front of the light and is projected onto a projector screen. As the movie plays, every single slide that is projected through the film projector is a sense of the present moment. So, the present is always moving. It never stops. Once the film has passed the projector light, it travels to the back reel, which is the past. The back reel is housing the part of the movie we have already seen.

Now, why do I bring up this? Everyone knows there's a future, a past, and a present. What you may not know is how those points of time have a SIGNIFICANT impact on your mindset. Do you recall the multitasking exercise? We can only focus on one thing at a time, thus, we can only be in one reference of time or another. This is the critical part. Let's dig further.

Let's say that you're watching a movie and in the present scene, a drunken man is seen ripping the front door open and running out of the house. He has his car keys in one hand and a beer bottle in the other. As you watch his every move, he runs to the car, pissed and drunk. He gets to the car, struggles with the door a bit, and gets in. He slams the beer bottle in the center console, shoves the key into the ignition, and starts the car. As he puts the car into reverse, he puts the pedal to the metal, backing out of the driveway as fast as he can. He then slams the car into drive and floors it, squealing tires as he takes off.

All of a sudden, your mind shifts, "Oh, my God, what's about to happen? What if this happens or that happens?" You might even be holding your head, saying, "Oh, my God, this is gonna get really, really bad." You begin to worry and get anxious. You're really concerned; you start to visualize what's going to happen as if you're a fortune teller! This desire to know what's next pushes you to shift your thinking to the future reel, that area storing the rest of the movie you have yet to see. Not knowing what's going to play out, you start imagining what might end up happening. This is where *anxiety* comes from. You shift from the present moment to the future. Since you can only process one thought at a time, when you move your single thought to that future wheel, you can no longer be present. When you aren't present—because you're focused on what's about to happen and literally not paying attention to the movie playing—you're missing the movie and everything that's happening at the moment. You visualize a really, really bad outcome for the drunk guy. "Oh, my God! He's going to kill someone!" However, in reality, you don't really know.

All of a sudden you snap back to the present moment! You've spent the last four or five minutes not paying any attention to the movie at hand—because if you're paying attention to the future, you cannot be paying attention to the movie that's actually playing—and you just realized you spent all that time thinking about what was about to happen. Your mindset shifts again back to the present moment. "Oh, my God, I just missed part of the movie." While you were fortune-telling about what could have happened, the movie you missed has now rolled up into your past. Now you shift again, this time to the past wheel. "If only I would have paid attention. If only I would have paid attention while the movie was playing, I would know what's going on. Instead, I just totally missed that." That's where we see *depression*. That's where you start to get sad or angry, all the while missing the movie as it is currently playing.

When you think about the future in an attempt to control it, one of the main questions you ask is, "What if this happens?" or, "What if that happens?" When things that we missed go to the past reel on the film projector, you start saying to yourself, "If only I had spent more time with my grandmother," or "I should have done this," or "I should have done that."

When it comes to time, recognize that anxiety is really future-based thinking and depression is historical past-based thinking—what has already happened. Many people will say they have anxiety or depression. They identify with it; however, anxiety or depression is not something you have. It is not a fever, a wart, or the chicken pox. Anxiety and depression is an experience; it is an effect of your thinking. This is key to removing any self-identification to anxiety and depression. Recognizing that, "I do not have anxiety; I experience it," is important so you can remove it without also experiencing an identity crisis.

So, anxiety is the experience of wanting to control the

future, yet we can't, while depression is the experience we feel when we regret not being present. Only when we focus on the present moment—the light coming through the film projector lens—can we ever find happiness. You may have heard it before, "The present is called the present because it is our gift," and it is our true gift. This is why we want to train our mindset to be consumed with the present moment and not jumping to conclusions about what's going to happen in the future or regretting what's in the past. Because, as they say, "It's water under the bridge." We're now in a new circumstance, a new situation, and we have to deal with the present moment as it is—we can't make it something that it's not. It is what it is.

Maybe you are the mother of a young son who is a few years old. Early on, you start hearing his pediatrician talking about the potential of him being autistic. Over and over, this word "autistic" is being spoken by his doctors to the point it is constantly bouncing around in your mind. "What if he is? Am I holding him back? What if he doesn't do well in school? Maybe the school I want him to go to won't accept him. Will people make fun of him?" Thinking about your son being autistic and his future before it happens leads you to restless nights, anxiety and uncontrollable tears. All the worrying about the future is doing nothing but robbing you of the precious moments of your little boy growing up. You don't even know yet whether he is truly autistic. Be in the moment; he needs you, and he loves you.

The next chapter will give us a tool that can enable our ability to manage how we deal with time, anxiety, and depression. For many people, it seems there's a great amount of underlying anxiousness that leads to negative behaviors.

REFLECTION, PREPARATION, AND MINDFULNESS

When you think about the past with regret, you become depressed. Likewise, worrying about the future causes anxiety. Only in the present moment can you live in happiness. That's how time influences your emotions.

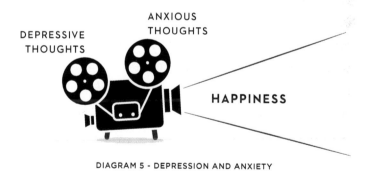

DIAGRAM 5 - DEPRESSION AND ANXIETY

Look at Diagram 5, "Depression and Anxiety." With a low-performing mindset, anxiety is caused by thinking about the future, and depression is caused by thinking about the past. Happiness is what's right in front of you—your present. You can't control the future or change the past, and when you dwell on them, you miss the opportunity for happiness in the moment. As I mentioned earlier, anxiety is a thinking error and an experience caused by our inability to control the future.

Since you can't control the future or change the past, focusing on those references of time with intentions to control or change them leads to anxiety and depression. I get it, though; someone might say, "I can't always live in the present, right? I've got to be able to think about what's going on ahead of us. I've got to do things so that the things in the future don't become problematic and to plan."

Let's be clear, the high performance mindset doesn't ignore the future or the past; it deals with each of them in a positive and present manner, without anxiety or depression.

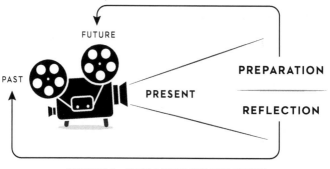

FUTURE

PAST

PRESENT

PREPARATION

REFLECTION

DIAGRAM 6 - PREPARATION AND REFLECTION

Diagram 6, "Preparation and Reflection," illustrates this concept. The truth is, when we are in the present moment, we can absolutely prepare for the future. This is not anxiety in the sense that I'm worried about what's going to happen. We do this with preparation and reflection. Preparation is planning for the future. When you prepare—when you're sitting at the kitchen counter preparing food for the evening meal—that is a present-moment activity. You're doing it right now and you're preparing for the meal that is about to come. So, in the present moment, we look at that future reel and we look at that front film projector wheel, and what we see is preparation. That's how we stay present—we're constantly preparing for what's coming. We're not worried about it or ruminating on it; we're preparing.

Focusing on the present while preparing for the future removes the anxiety that's typically associated with future events in two ways. First, it shifts your focus from the future to the present. You cannot be anxious when your thoughts are in the present, because anxiety is an emotion that's tied to future thoughts.

Second, preparation puts you in a better position to manage future events. In the film projector example, you choose to view the future reel as an opportunity for preparation. Then you can focus on present activities that prepare you for the future. Completing those activities will help to ensure a more positive outcome for your future. Again, this decreases your anxiety.

The same concept is true for the reel of film on the back of the projector—your past. A low-performing mindset focuses on the past with regret and depression. If you start worrying about the things that you missed, like spending time with your grandmother who passed away, or giving your ex-girlfriend or ex-boyfriend more of your time, you say, "They left me because I didn't give them enough time and now I see that." You can stay present while looking at the back reel in reflection. You can reflect back and ask, "How could I have done this differently so that in the future, if this happens again, I know how to handle it?" I call that reflection, but it's also introspection. It's self-awareness to recognize what's going on with you in your present state by understanding how you feel, or how that breakup felt because you didn't do everything that you should have done to save the relationship. You need to learn from that, and how *do* you learn from that? You learn through reflection and introspection. Look back on historical information and ask yourself, "Where could I have improved?" Note that improvement and drive that forward. "I am going to take better care of my bills and improve my credit so I am not denied again." This allows you to become a better person as you are preparing for your future, all within the present state.

You have a choice in where your mindset goes. You can certainly be upset at the past. "I am upset with the fact that I didn't get to see my grandfather before he passed away or my grandmother before she passed away." Or, you can choose to reflect and say, "You know what? At least she imprinted on my life." That's the power of reflection. "I'll look back at all the things that my grandmother taught me before she passed away. I can't be more thankful and appreciative for what she taught me, and I will ensure her legacy lives on."

That's what high-performance mindsets are about.

Remember, there are only three references of time. There's the future, the present, and the past. Like I said before, we only have one thought at a time. If you're anxious, you can't be depressed. If you're depressed, you can't be anxious. If you're present, you can't be anxious or depressed. So where do we want to be? Be in the present moment, preparing and reflecting, while using introspection and self-awareness to continue to improve. You apply your thoughts, focus, self-talk, attention, and concentration toward any of the three references of time—past, present, or future. Use your present thoughts to deal with the past and the future in a way that benefits you.

In Chapter 5, I'll provide you with a tool that enables you to manage how your mind deals with negative biases that are based on memories of the past. These biases can creep into your thoughts and cause negative behavior in the present.

DEALING WITH NEGATIVE AND SELF-DEFEATING THOUGHTS

As we mentioned in the cause and effect discussion in Chapter 3, we do not have neutral thoughts. This chapter is going to focus on the 80 percent of our thoughts each day that are negative. Interestingly enough, we remember very few of our actual thoughts. However, we will always remember how they made us feel. If you recall, thought drives emotion. You may not realize that you had a bunch of negative thoughts yesterday; however, if you know you had a "bad day," that's a sign that you spent most of the day stuck in negative thinking. The same goes for having a great day. You probably will not recall your thoughts; however, you know they were more positive than negative.

Your subconscious mind and all its past experiences are responsible for this negativity. The subconscious mind stores pieces of your experiences to make recall happen faster. That way, your subconscious mind can tell your conscious mind what it knows quickly and without having to work very hard.

Your subconscious mind looks for similarities between experiences and makes generalizations about them. Once it has identified a pattern between experiences, it creates a generalization between the experiences. To the subconscious mind, that generalization becomes your truth. Your truth, as flawed as it may be, is what your subconscious mind uses to influence your conscious mind about what it is experiencing in order to protect you. Since your conscious mind identifies thoughts as positive or negative based upon the information it receives from your subconscious mind, you can see how your subconscious mind and its flawed beliefs are responsible for so many negative thoughts. And as a result of your subconscious mind's potential inaccuracy, your conscious mind might make decisions based on bad information.

Your thoughts truly determine your destiny. So, when you *allow* your thoughts to be based on bad information, you're relinquishing power over your life to your subconscious mind and the bad information it's giving your conscious mind, which usually results in negative thoughts and negative results.

Nothing positive comes from a negative thought. Negative thoughts have negative outcomes. Period. They prevent you from creating a framework for success in business, sports, and life. They limit your ability to grow and develop, and they keep you from absolutely crushing it!

However, you can tip the scale in your favor—increase the positive thoughts and decrease the negative ones—by taking actions to alter what your subconscious mind tells your conscious mind. To do this, you have to debate your existing beliefs and then create new positive beliefs to replace the old, outdated beliefs—all those truths you've accepted that are really just invalid generalizations of many individual experiences.

You don't have to settle for 80 percent negative thoughts and 20 percent positive thoughts. To have a high performance mindset, you must improve this percentage. You can retrain your subconscious mind to reevaluate its truths, question their validity, and adopt new beliefs. You can change how you think about things and, in doing so, begin to see everything in a more positive light.

Negativity is so prevalent in our society that you may not

even notice it. This is somewhat the human default state in that the mind is always seeking to protect us so we can survive, not thrive. No one talks about the thousands of planes that made successful flights today. Instead, the media covers the story about the one plane that crashed. You don't see stories of the thousands of officers who saved lives; you see the one that went rogue. That's what people are drawn to—the negative story. However, you can rewire your brain to "buck the system" and see the positive side of life. There's a silver lining in absolutely every situation. With training, you can go from an 80/20 ratio of negative to positive, to a 70/30 and even a 50/50. Can you imagine how much your life would change if half your thoughts, focus, self-talk, attention, and concentration were positive? How might that change your day-to-day existence? How would making half of your thoughts positive alter your destiny?

The possibilities are mindboggling, and it all starts with rewriting your subconscious truths—those irrational beliefs you've developed in your lifetime that cloud your conscious thoughts and hold you back from the life you've been wanting so badly. By challenging yourself to question those beliefs, you can uncover the truth and open yourself to the many possibilities available to you.

DR. ALBERT ELLIS'S CATEGORIES OF IRRATIONAL BELIEFS

The irrational beliefs that people develop tend to fall within seven categories, which were identified many years ago by Dr. Albert Ellis.[5] You might identify some of your own irrational beliefs within these categories.

DEMANDINGNESS AND ABSOLUTISM

Absolutes and demands use words and phrases like *should*, *always, never*, and *must*. When you adopt an absolute about something based on a generalization of past experiences, you cling to that belief and project it onto similar things, people, events, or situations in the present.

In essence, you create a biased assumption that isn't true. For example, thinking, "I must get what I want." Or, if your friend has a child and every time you're around that child, you see him act out. You might create an irrational belief that your friend's child always acts out and is bad. However, you could be wrong. Maybe you just saw him when he was acting out, while in reality, he's usually well behaved. However, in your mind, you've already decided, "My friend's child always acts out."

---

5   Albert Ellis and Shaun Blau, *A Guide to Well-Being Using Rational Emotive Behavior Therapy* (New York: Citadel Press, 1998).

Always is an absolute, because it means every single time. However, how many things *always* happen? The word *never* is also an absolute, because it means not one single time. And again, how often do these words really apply? In reality, absolutes are rare. Yet, some people readily adopt an absolute perspective about the people, places, events, and situations in their lives. Does that sound rational? It's not rational. Remember when we talked about the power of the words we use? Using absolutes, like the confusion of linguistics, can create beliefs that aren't true.

DEMAND FOR LOVE AND APPROVAL

The second category of irrational beliefs is the demand for love and approval from everyone who's important to you. Is it fair to expect someone to approve of you or even love you because they matter to you? That's not a rational demand, and if you have that expectation, you're setting yourself up for disappointment—and a lot of negative thoughts.

DEMAND FOR SUCCESS OR ACHIEVEMENT

The third category of irrational beliefs is a demand for success or achievement in everything that's important to you. Some people place so much importance on success, they're paralyzed by the thought of failure, so they don't even strive to succeed.

DEMAND FOR COMFORT AND LOW TOLERANCE FOR DISCOMFORT

Most people have a demand for comfort and a very low tolerance for discomfort. This is the fourth category of irrational beliefs. However, when you're comfortable, you're not growing, and so this demand for comfort is irrational. It prevents you from learning. Putting yourself in new and uncomfortable situations is necessary for growth.

AWFULIZATION

The fifth category of irrational beliefs is awfulization. This refers to the tendency to focus on the worst-case scenario of every situation. Do you have a friend whose life seems to be in constant upheaval and everything about their existence is a disaster? People with awfulization beliefs think their lives are much worse than everyone else's and they will argue with you to prove it.

LOW FRUSTRATION TOLERANCE

Low frustration tolerance, the sixth category, is characterized by the irrational belief that everything is difficult. Do you know someone who sees everything as an insurmountable challenge? If they understood that their frustration was based on irrational expectations, they could adjust their expectations and, in effect, lower their level of frustration. Remember, we talked earlier about the cause of frustration being unmet expectations.

THE GLOBAL RATING

The final category of irrational beliefs, according to Dr. Ellis, is the global rating. This is the tendency to assign a derogatory label to a person. Do you know someone who's a stupid, worthless idiot? Are they really? Although they may have done something stupid, as a human does, they're surely making some kind of contribution to society. People tend to assign global ratings to other people who cause them problems. This actually ends up putting the burden of weight on the person making that irrational judgment. Global ratings create stereotypes that can have a negative impact on your mindset.

Your negative thoughts—the 80 percent of all your thinking on average—are mainly due to irrational beliefs within these seven categories. Now that you know where they come from, let's talk about how they affect you.

THE EFFECTS OF IRRATIONAL BELIEFS

The irrational beliefs stored in your subconscious mind heavily influence your conscious mind and your life. These beliefs limit your capability, your happiness, and your overall level of success. They can quickly distort the way you see the world, create negative emotions, and drive self-defeating behaviors.

This is commonly referred to as "baby elephant syndrome." Let me tell you a story. One day, a baby elephant was purchased and brought to the circus. To keep the elephant from running away, the elephant trainer wrapped a chain around the baby elephant's leg and attached the chain to a stick in the ground. After the trainer walked away, the elephant attempted to get away several times. However, he was unable to break the chain or pull the stick from the ground. He kept at it. After a while, he stopped pulling on the chain—even when he became a fully grown, powerful adult elephant.

One day a fire broke out in the circus. As the fire quickly surrounded the elephant, he could have easily broken the chain with his strength and run away from the circus; however, he didn't. Even though he could have saved himself, he instead died in the fire because he still believed he couldn't break that chain.

That's an example of how irrational beliefs can affect your behavior. You might have attempted something at one point in your life, and if you didn't achieve your expected outcome, you gave up and never attempted to reach that goal again. Or maybe you didn't believe you would be successful, so when you made an attempt and didn't find success, it strengthened your existing belief. You accepted the results, thus allowing your limiting beliefs to "kill" your opportunities for success.

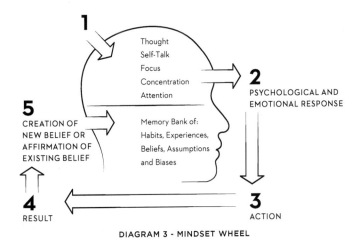

DIAGRAM 3 - MINDSET WHEEL

Going back to Diagram 3, "Mindset Wheel," your conscious thoughts emerge from subconscious conditioning. In the case of the baby elephant, he attempted to break the chain and rip the stick out of the ground. He couldn't do it, so his belief became, "I can't move this thing. I'm stuck here and can't go anywhere." Similar beliefs occur to people in their everyday lives. Metaphorically speaking, there may not be a chain or a stick holding you back; however, other factors appear as barriers to your freedom.

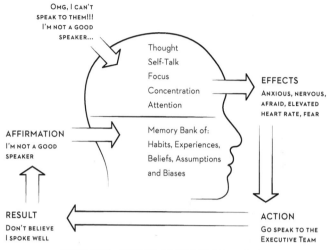

WILL YOU SPEAK TO OUR EXECUTIVE LEADERSHIP TEAM
TOMORROW ABOUT THE GREAT WORK YOU HAVE BEEN DOING?

OMG, I CAN'T
SPEAK TO THEM!!!
I'M NOT A GOOD
SPEAKER...

Thought
Self-Talk
Focus
Concentration
Attention

EFFECTS
ANXIOUS, NERVOUS,
AFRAID, ELEVATED
HEART RATE, FEAR

AFFIRMATION
I'M NOT A GOOD
SPEAKER

Memory Bank of:
Habits, Experiences,
Beliefs, Assumptions
and Biases

RESULT
DON'T BELIEVE
I SPOKE WELL

ACTION
GO SPEAK TO THE
EXECUTIVE TEAM

DIAGRAM 7 - EFFECTS OF IRRATIONAL THOUGHTS

For an example of how irrational thoughts can limit you, let's look at Diagram 7, "Effects of Irrational Thoughts." Imagine that your boss asked you to speak to the executive team. He wants you to talk to them about the great work you've been doing. Immediately, your conscious mind asks your subconscious mind, "What do you know about speaking?" Your subconscious mind then pulls up anything regarding speaking from your past.

If in the past, you have spoken in front of a group, and you didn't feel the speech went well, your subconscious mind answers you and tells you that you stink at speaking. Then, your initial thought, self-talk, and focus might go something like this: "Oh, no! I can't speak to them. I'm not a good speaker. I can hardly talk in front of my own group! How am I supposed to talk to the leaders of my organization?"

Those negative thoughts generate negative physiological and emotional responses. Your heart's beating in your chest, your palms get sweaty, and you're anxious, nervous, and afraid. Although you don't want to do it, your boss is counting on you. Consumed by feelings of gloom and doom, you force yourself to speak to the executives. All those negative thoughts, responses, and emotions get in the way. Your voice trembles, your hands shake, and you lose your train of thought. The speech is a disaster. The results confirm what you knew all along—you're a bad speaker. Thus, you harden up the existing subconscious belief that you suck at speaking.

When your mindset is based on irrational beliefs, those beliefs influence your actions and the negative results fortify those beliefs. No matter how irrational your beliefs are, the results of your actions make you believe them even more.

With a low-performing mindset, you create more of your current mindset. Each time you test your irrational beliefs, you reinforce them with negative results, and they become more ingrained in your subconscious mind. Over time, it becomes harder and harder to dispel them.

However, you *can* dispel them. You can eradicate your irrational beliefs and free yourself from the negative thoughts that influence your behaviors and responses and limit your actions. With the high performance mindset, it doesn't matter what you believe about yourself now, because you can change it. It only matters that you're ready to make a change and willing to put in the work. Everything worth having requires work.

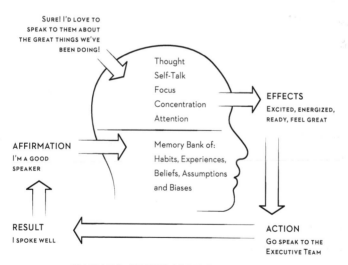

WILL YOU SPEAK TO OUR EXECUTIVE LEADERSHIP TEAM TOMORROW ABOUT THE GREAT WORK YOU HAVE BEEN DOING?

SURE! I'D LOVE TO SPEAK TO THEM ABOUT THE GREAT THINGS WE'VE BEEN DOING!

Thought
Self-Talk
Focus
Concentration
Attention

EFFECTS
EXCITED, ENERGIZED, READY, FEEL GREAT

AFFIRMATION
I'M A GOOD SPEAKER

Memory Bank of:
Habits, Experiences,
Beliefs, Assumptions
and Biases

RESULT
I SPOKE WELL

ACTION
GO SPEAK TO THE EXECUTIVE TEAM

DIAGRAM 8 - EFFECTS OF RATIONAL THOUGHTS

Let's see how the same scenario would play out with a high performance mindset. Look at Diagram 8, "Effects of Rational Thoughts." In this example, you've replaced that old, negative belief with a new, positive one: "I'm a good speaker." Now, when your boss asks you to speak to the executive team, your response reflects your new belief and you respond with, "Sure, I'd love to speak to them about the great work I'm doing!"

You're excited to address the team and you enthusiastically prepare a speech. When the day comes for you to speak, your energy and enthusiasm are reflected in your demeanor, your posture, your body language, and your voice. You speak confidently and receive a standing ovation. You're a hit!

Your great speech and the positive outcome reinforce your new belief about yourself: You are a good speaker.

Several concepts are at work here. First, your subconscious belief about yourself changed, and that changed your conscious thoughts and your focus. Instead of focusing on that old, irrational belief that you're a poor speaker, you focused on a new belief of yourself as a good speaker. Then, your positive belief affected your emotional and physiological responses in a positive manner, which changed your behavior. Remember, thoughts drive emotion, emotions drive action, and actions drive results. In this example, your results are that you performed well and received positive feedback, reinforcing that positive belief.

You also chose to think about the future through preparation instead of anxiety. You did all that by changing your subconscious beliefs about yourself. So, does that mean the key to the high performance mindset is a matter of controlling your subconscious mind?

It's not quite that simple! You can't control your subconscious mind at will. As I mentioned before, your subconscious mind is always listening, recording information, and forming generalizations. You can't stop that process.

To develop a high performance mindset, you have to question your thoughts and be willing to dispel them if they aren't true. However, those thoughts are based on your beliefs, and beliefs are powerful things. Think about your religious and political beliefs. What would it take to change them? They are most likely pretty concrete. What if, knowing you're a Republican, I told you all kinds of bad things about Republicans and tried to convince you to switch parties? Painful, right? In fact, when we receive information that conflicts with our beliefs, we chuck them.

Don't worry, I'm not asking you to change your religion or your political party. However, the same holds true for your other beliefs. To you, they're the truth, plain and simple. Also at play here is what is called confirmation bias: We seek out that which matches our beliefs.

Now do you see why questioning your irrational thoughts can be difficult? You're going to get uncomfortable. Growing and learning demand that you get at least *a little* uncomfortable. To change your mindset, you have to be willing to entertain new thoughts and ideas. Instead of accepting the truths you've been telling yourself all your life, you have to consider that some of those truths aren't true. So, how bad do you want a better life? Good, keep reading!

Other beliefs you have may be just as deeply ingrained in your subconscious as your politics, religious views, and your personal values—and as difficult to question. Self-talk is your key to challenging your beliefs. That conversation that constantly runs in your head *is* your thoughts and that conversation *is* under your control; taking charge of it can change your focus and your life. Once you've changed your beliefs about yourself, you have to test them. Testing your beliefs will help to deliver positive results that help to reinforce your new, positive beliefs in your subconscious mind. Creating the habit is key.

REAL-LIFE SELF-TALK: TESTING THE NEW MINDSET

When you learn something new, you have to apply it in order for your new knowledge to "stick." It's the same with a new mindset. Once you've changed a belief about yourself, you have to put that new belief into action. Testing your positive beliefs about yourself reinforces them.

I learned this firsthand when I was asked to teach hospital employees about HIPAA, the Health Insurance Portability and Accountability Act. HIPAA is a set of rules that people who handle medical records have to follow to ensure patients' privacy. The language around HIPAA is tricky and can be confusing for anyone who's new to compliance rules.

Every month, I had to provide an hour-long orientation presentation. I started by orienting two people at a time, then three, then twenty, and eventually I worked up to training forty people at a time. At first, I was scared to death. My self-talk was, "I don't know what I'm doing. This is going to be horrible." It's a good thing I was only working with a couple of people that first time because the training was horrible! I was a disaster. There was a huge knot in my throat, I was sweating, breathing erratically, and stumbling over my words. My audience was confused and bored. I realized that I had to change my self-talk and my belief about my presentation abilities.

As I began to change my self-talk, my beliefs changed and my HIPAA training sessions improved. I received improved results and positive feedback that reinforced my new beliefs. Eventually, my mindset around training people about HIPAA changed completely.

It didn't happen overnight. I had to accept that I wasn't the best HIPAA presenter out there; however, I was good enough and I could get even better. My self-talk changed to, "I need to keep honing my presentation to the point that it's easy for me to explain and easy for people to understand. I need to make it interesting too, so my audience doesn't fall asleep on me." I got better—so much better that I looked forward to the orientations. I made the training fun and easy for everyone to understand. As crazy as it may sound, I was eventually able to present the training well enough that the staff I was training gave me a lot of positive, unsolicited recognition for a fun training program.

Changing your beliefs requires more than simply changing your self-talk, and we'll discuss how to change your irrational beliefs in the next chapter. Changing your beliefs allows you to change your thoughts, your focus, your attention, your concentration—and your life.

PART II

MINDSET SHIFT TOOLS

CHAPTER 06

MINDSET SHIFT TOOL 1: CREATE NEW POSITIVE BELIEFS

Four techniques, which I call "Mindset Shift Tools," comprise this program that will help you develop the high performance mindset. Each one is easy to learn and requires no special tools beyond a notebook, a pen, and a willingness to develop a better, faster, and more efficient mental mindset.

With the first tool, you'll replace negative, irrational thoughts with powerful, positive beliefs. This is key to reversing the negative effects discussed in the previous chapter where we talked about changing your self-talk so you can excel at your next presentation. You'll learn how to create affirmations and initiate a new dialogue with yourself—a dialogue of positive, self-affirming statements to change your beliefs.

You can use this tool to debate the 80 percent of your thoughts that aren't beneficial to you. As you shift from a ratio of 80/20 negative/positive thoughts to a ratio of 70/30, and as more of your repetitive thoughts are positive ones, you'll move forward in a more positive direction. The world of the positive thinker is empowering, open, and available. That world is here, waiting for you. You just have to know how to ask for it.

THE ABCDE TECHNIQUE

Mindset Shift Tool 1: "Create New Positive Beliefs," is based on rational emotive behavioral coaching, developed by Dr. Ellis. His ABCDE technique is the basis of the single most important tool I've ever used. I changed several aspects of the tool as I noticed gaps with my clients. The end result is a very effective tool for anyone who has an emotional pain point in their life, from anxiety and depression to anger, frustration, and irritability. These emotions keep you from having positive thoughts and limit your abilities. This mindset shift tool is a way to hack into your subconscious so you can debate your negative thoughts and create new beliefs about yourself—and new truths within your subconscious mind.

My ABCDE technique is quite profound, because it's worked for me and for the people I coach *every single time.* Remember, I promised that my tools were consistent. They worked for us and they'll work for you.

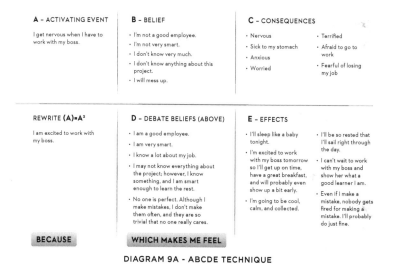

DIAGRAM 9A - ABCDE TECHNIQUE

This mindset shift tool requires just two sheets of paper and a pen. Follow these seven steps to complete the exercise, illustrated in Diagram 9A, "ABCDE Technique."

EXERCISE 3: THE ABCDE TECHNIQUE

STEP ONE

Turn the first piece of paper sideways to landscape orientation. Draw two vertical lines, dividing the paper into three columns. Label, at the top, the first column A, the second column B, and the third column C. A stands for "Activating Event," B is for "Belief," and C is for "Consequences."

STEP TWO

Column A

In this column, write your activating event. This is a single event that triggers your anxiety, depression, anger, frustration, irritability, or any other negative emotion.

As an example of this technique, pretend that you have to work alongside your boss on a project tomorrow. You don't normally work side by side with her. You don't know that much about the project and you're worried that you're going to mess up. Thinking about tomorrow has you feeling anxious, and you probably won't get much sleep tonight. You may even call in sick to keep from working with your boss. This is a good example of how you can change your perspective, your beliefs, and your attitude with a mindset shift tool.

In this example, you might write: *I get nervous when I have to work with my boss* in the A column.

Column B

In this column, write your beliefs about the activating event that are making you nervous. Why are you nervous about working with your boss? You might write the following:

- *I'm not a good employee.*
- *I'm not very smart.*
- *I don't know very much.*
- *I don't know anything about this project.*
- *I will mess up.*

You don't have to stop at four items. If there are more, keep writing! Get it all out there. This could spark some emotion. That's okay, because at times emotion is necessary to get everything you're thinking and feeling out. Although you need to be as thorough as possible, make your statements simple and precise. Don't leave any stone unturned.

Column C

In this column, the C column, write down the conse-quences of these beliefs. How do the beliefs in column B make you feel? Write down all the consequences in column C.

For example, you might write:

- *Nervous*
- *Sick to my stomach*
- *Anxious*
- *Worried*
- *Terrified*
- *Afraid to go to work*
- *Fearful of losing my job*

Whatever the consequences of your beliefs are, be sure to fully document them. Now lift the paper up in the air. Look at it and read it out loud as a statement.

Read A, then say "because," then read B, then say, "which makes me feel," then read C. For this example, you will say: "I get nervous when I have to work with my boss *because* I am not a good employee, I am not smart, I do not know very much, I don't know anything about this project, and I will mess up *which makes me feel* nervous, sick to my stomach, anxious, worried, terrified, afraid to go to work, and fearful of losing my job."

Is this an accurate representation of your issue? If not, rework it until it describes your situation. Let's move on to the next step.

STEP THREE

Next, lay that piece of paper down and slide it away from you. Get out another piece of paper. Turn it sideways and draw two vertical lines on it, just like the first one. Label these three columns A2, D, and E. D stands for "Debate" and E is for "Effects." We'll get to A2 in a few minutes.

STEP FOUR

Read the first belief in column B, *I'm not a good employee.* Now, ask yourself if that belief is true. Are you really not a good employee?

Think about it. Debate it. You go to work every day, right? Have you had any successes at work? Have you accomplished anything? Has your boss every complimented you? When you imagine a known "bad employee," do you see yourself in that role? You probably don't, and in fact, you're probably a good employee, aren't you?

Column D

Now, on your second sheet of paper, in the second column, column D, I want you to write as you debate the beliefs you wrote in column B. As you discover the truth about those beliefs, write down your new belief in column D. For example, *I am a good employee.* Now go to the next belief, *I'm not very smart.* Debate it. Are you really not very smart? Think about all that you've learned and all you know. You're probably very smart. Think about someone who you feel is not very smart. Is that really you? Not likely. Write your new belief in column D, *I am smart.*

Continue until you've debated every one of your old, irrational, negative beliefs and written the truth about yourself in column D. Sometimes, you'll have a belief that's honest. In this case, just copy it to D. Your Column D might look like this:

- *I am a good employee.*
- *I am very smart.*
- *I know a lot about my job.*
- *I may not know everything about this project; however, I know something and I'm smart enough to learn the rest.*
- *No one is perfect. Although I make mistakes, I don't make them often and they're so trivial that no one cares.*

Look at that list. That's you! That's who you really are—your uncovered, rational and real truths.

Column E

Now go to the third column, "Effects." What are the effects of column D: Knowing the truth about yourself? Write them down. They should look very different than column C on your first sheet of paper. In fact, they might even be the exact opposite of everything on that list. Your new list might be something like this:

- *I'll sleep like a baby tonight.*
- *I'm excited to work with my boss tomorrow so I'll get up on time, have a great breakfast, and will probably even show up a bit early.*
- *I'm going to be cool, calm, and collected.*
- *I'll be so rested that I'll sail right through the day.*
- *I can't wait to work with my boss and show her what a good learner I am.*
- *Even if I make a mistake, nobody gets fired for making a mistake. I'll probably do just fine.*

STEP FIVE

Okay, now go back to the first column on your first sheet of paper and that activating statement:

I get nervous when I have to work with my boss.

On your second sheet of paper, in the first column, A2, write your new activating event. This is your new belief and it's the *opposite* of what you wrote in column A.

Column A2

Write, *I am excited to work with my boss.*

Then below that, write the word *because* in a box.

You should have something that looks like this:

I am excited to work with my boss.

- -

    Because:

- -

In column D, below your debates, write "which makes me feel" in a box. You should have something like this:

Column D

- *I'm a good employee.*
- *I'm excited to work with my boss.*

- *I'm cool, calm, and collected at work.*
- *I can sail right through the day.*
- *I enjoy showing her what a good learner I am.*
- *Even if I make a mistake, nobody gets fired for making a mistake and I will do just fine!*

- -

Which makes me feel

- -

By combining your new activating event with your new *because* statements and your new *which makes me feel* statements, you'll have an affirmation statement that describes your new belief. For example, your new belief might be:

I am excited to work with my boss because I'm a good employee, which makes me feel cool, calm, collected, and confident. I'm smart and I know a lot about my job, so I enjoy working alongside my boss. Even if I make an occasional mistake, it's okay. I'm human and everyone makes mistakes. No one at work has ever been fired for making a mistake and I have nothing to be nervous about.

STEP SIX

Read your new belief out loud. How does it make you feel? You should feel great, or at least a lot better than before you started this mindset shift tool! That's the real you, the high performance mindset you!

Now it's time to take the first piece of paper and get rid of it. From a symbolic perspective, we want to visualize its destruction. It's not who you are and has no place in your life. Crumple it up, shred it, or burn it. You may have heard the term "controlled burn." Landowners often use controlled burning to create new growth. When I coach clients through this tool, I prefer for them to burn the first piece of paper to create new growth mentally. Say goodbye to that old version of who you used to be. Do it and say, "I AM DONE WITH YOU!"

STEP SEVEN

The second page has now become your affirmation statement. Say this out loud, looking in a mirror, three times a day for at least two weeks. If the issue is something that's about to happen and less than two weeks away, verbalize your affirmation as many times as you can between now and then. Read it first thing in the morning. This affirmation needs to be the first thing you say to yourself. If you post it on the bathroom mirror, you'll see it when you brush your teeth and you won't forget. Look yourself in the eyes in the mirror and say your affirmation loud and clear. Mean it. This is important.

Bring your affirmation to work with you and find a private place at lunchtime to look in a mirror—in the bathroom at work, in your car, or at home—and read it again. Finally, read it out loud a third time before you go to bed, again, looking at yourself in the mirror. Make it the last thing you say to yourself before you go to bed each night.

You're giving your subconscious mind new information, which it turns into beliefs. This is how you train your subconscious to adopt new beliefs about yourself.

★ ★ ★

The ABCDE technique creates affirmations specific to your beliefs and helps you overcome irrational thoughts and replaces them with positive, rational thoughts. By verbalizing these affirmations and using your self-talk to remind yourself of your affirmations, you can hack your subconscious mind and change its truths.

Once you change your subconscious mind, you change the information it gives your conscious mind about how to think and feel about everything—people, places, things, situations, and experiences.

By exposing your irrational thoughts, you can get to the source of everything that's holding you back. Then, you can meet those invisible barriers head-on, challenge their validity, and rewrite the outcome of your activating event. You can express positive, empowering thoughts that change your beliefs about yourself and move you closer to the high performance mindset.

Is there an event that triggers your anxiety, depression, anger, or frustration? While it can be work- or sports-related—like working with your boss or competing in a race—it doesn't have to be. Your activating event can be anything from taking a test to driving on the freeway or asking a girl out on a date. All kinds of events can trigger negative emotions, and the ABCDE technique can be employed whenever you need to replace your irrational thoughts with positive beliefs. Use it! I'm telling you, it's the best tool I've ever utilized, and it works every time. Then come back and read Chapter 7. We're going to talk about the kick-ass you.

REAL-LIFE ABCDE EXAMPLES

The ABCDE technique helps my sports clients deal with anxieties and get better results. To illustrate the process and effects, here are two examples of real clients who were preparing for an Ironman Triathlon. Real-Life ABCDE Examples

The ABCDE technique helps my sports clients deal with anxieties and get better results. To illustrate the process and effects, here are two examples of real clients who were preparing for an Ironman Triathlon.

An Ironman combines three events. While there are shorter variations, a full Ironman includes a 2.4-mile swim followed by a 112-mile bicycling event and a 26.22-mile marathon run. In a full Ironman, athletes are moving nonstop for around eight to sixteen hours without any sort of music device. Let's be honest, that's a lot of time to be spending "in your own head." Your thoughts can be your greatest asset or your largest liability.

Ironman competitions have time limits for each event and for the overall race. While athletes always want to achieve their personal best time in any race, anyone who completes the race within the time limit crosses the finish line to a cheering crowd, and is proclaimed over the intercom, "You are an Ironman!"

In the first example, "Real-Life Example of Fear of Failure and the ABCDE Technique," John came to me with a lot of anxiety. Through our conversations, I discovered that John had an underlying fear of failure. Anxiety is caused by our inability to control the future. It is often irrational thoughts based on past events—or the unknown—that manifest when we think about the uncertain future through that negative filter. We used the ABCDE technique to help him deal with this anxiety.

John's activating event was a fear of failing in the Ironman event. He wrote that fear in his A column: I'm afraid of failing the Ironman. Then I asked John to tell me what was making him anxious. John told me that he believed he would never be a successful athlete. He said that no one would describe him as an athlete. John didn't see himself as athletic and that was creating anxiety for him as he trained for the race. He also said that he'd trained for ten months and hadn't made any progress. That didn't surprise me because athletes who train every day tend to look for changes every day. Those changes are so subtle that athletes sometimes don't realize that, over time, they are making progress. John's day-to-day improvement wasn't obvious to him; however, if he paid attention to his tracked progress from week to week or month

month, he would feel more confident about his development. This
a common oversight for many people; even the greatest athletes
uggle with this at times.

John told me that everything he wanted seemed to escape him. That
told me that John felt victimized. His subconscious mind had, at some
point in time, been trained to believe he was a bystander and it affected
how he approached all of his goals. Unable to take a positive approach,
he felt that he was fighting an invisible force that was keeping him
from getting what he wanted in life. Finally, John believed there were
people who didn't want him to do well in the Ironman, and who would
celebrate his failure. Although that was likely a distorted vision of how
the people around him actually felt, it was his truth. He believed it.

John's worst fear was that he wouldn't complete the race within a
certain time. That was a major clue to his anxiety. John had never run
a full Ironman before, yet he expected to finish the race with a fast
time. That was an unreasonable expectation, yet he had imposed it
upon himself and now he was stressed out because he didn't believe he
could achieve it. Remember what we said about unmet expectations:
They lead to negative outcomes.

His outcome expectation caused him great animosity. When it comes
to setting outcomes for a race, many factors come into play during
the event that render the outcome beyond the control of an individual.
An athlete could get a flat tire during the biking section or pull a leg
muscle during the run. The weather—wind, rain, heat, cold, and humid-
ity—changes, or you could have stomach problems. The outcome is
beyond your control, and so a better tactic is to focus on what is within
your control in the race. Prepare mentally and physically, train, and
give it all you've got. Then accept the outcome—your time—knowing
that you did everything within your control to have the best possible
time. However, John had already decided that if he didn't finish the
race within a specific time, he would be a poor finisher.

The fact is, when you complete an Ironman, the t-shirt and medal you
get do not say "poor Ironman finisher." It just says that you finished,
because that's all that most people care about. When you cross the line,
the announcer doesn't say, "Congratulations, John, you suck because
you are slow!" Instead, the announcer says, "John! You ARE an Ironman!"

An outsider can easily see how his fears were caused by irrational beliefs.
However, they were his beliefs, deeply rooted in his subconscious
mind and affecting his conscious thoughts, and thus his emotions,
actions, and results.

As a high performance mindset coach, it's important for me to meet my clients where they are and accept their truths as reality—at first. I allowed his truths about himself to become my truths about him, as well.

We talked about the consequences of John's beliefs. He was nervous, nauseous, and losing sleep over the upcoming race. He believed that finishing it with a bad time would validate his belief that he wasn't an athlete. It would reinforce his poor self-image and confirm that he wasn't a winner.

We wrote all of this down in A, B, and C columns. I showed it to John. "Is this you?" I asked him. "Yup," he said, "that's me."

(A) ACTIVATING EVENT

- The thought of failing in the Half and Full Ironman makes me anxious.

(B) BELIEFS THAT CAUSE THE ANXIETY

- I have never been or will I ever be a successful athlete. No one would ever describe me as athletic.

- Although I have trained hard for almost ten months, I see no progress. I have not improved at all. Everything I really want always escapes me. The Ironman will be no different. Some people would celebrate me failing the Ironman. I will fail, and they will celebrate. It always happens.

- It's just not going to happen. Who am I kidding.

- I have never run an official Half Marathon or Full Marathon and everyone asks me if I have done these two. They know I'm trying to be an ironman, therefore, when they ask and I say no, they are telling me I'm sure to fail.

- I'm sure to hit a wall on the run and will be humiliated by not being able to finish the race.

- If I complete the race in more than seven hours for the Half Marathon or more than 15 hours in the Full Marathon, I really will not be an ironman. I will be a less than an ironman always with the caveat that I am an ironman who finished poorly.

(C) CONSEQUENCES BECAUSE OF THESE BELIEFS

- Nauseous

- Validation that I am not a winner

- Poor performance

- Nervousness

- Difficulty sleeping

- Mental games with self-effecting relationships and work

- Poor self-image

Then we went through the next steps of the ABCDE technique, A2, D, and E. I asked John about each of his beliefs, had him debate them and diffuse them. John discovered that he didn't need other people to believe he was an athlete. He realized that he had trained hard for a long time and had every right to see himself as an athlete. John was running five to ten miles a week and competing in 5K races. His time improved in each race, and he'd even completed one in negative thirty degree temperatures. He admitted that he'd also improved his time in two sprint races that year, and his overall sprint times by an average of twenty minutes. John had learned about all the components on his bike and how to change his tires. His stats showed that his biking and swimming times had improved, too.

(D) DIFFUSE BELIEFS ABOVE

- I don't need others to believe I'm an athlete or athletic. I have put in more time than most people have, so call it athletic or whatever, the word doesn't matter—the facts do.

- I have done better in the two sprints that I did last year and improved my time by an average of more than twenty minutes. I have run in more 5K's and have seen myself improve in all of those. I am a much better swimmer than I was a year ago. The stats are proof. I have improved my cycling through rigorous training with real cyclists who have made noticeable improvements. I understand CAD, Power and gears. I even changed the tires on my bike by myself and understand components. I have gone from never running to running a minimum of five to ten miles a week, and I participated in 5K events even in -30 degrees and completed.

- I have experienced success. I am a successful father. I have been a successful sales person with a great company. I have lived through abuse and have not resorted to believing I'm less than a person. The Ironman won't be any different. I am successful. I am a champion.

- If I do fail, at least I tried. I refuse to say I can't do it. I went out there and worked towards what I wanted. Those who would celebrate my defeat, which WILL NOT HAPPEN, don't matter and have no place in my life.

Once John debated each of his beliefs and focused on the facts rather than his irrational thoughts, he realized that he had made progress. In fact, he had excelled. We talked about his other successes. In his personal life, he was a great father. He had a successful career as a salesman. Although John had been successful in many parts of his life, he'd never given himself credit for any of it. By the end of the exercise, John realized he had nothing to fear. He was going to compete, give it his all, and accept the outcome. Regardless of how fast he ran, biked, and swam, he could finish the Ironman and be an Ironman finisher. He had nothing to fear.

(E) EFFECTS OF NEW BELIEFS

- I will be more confident.

- It doesn't matter what others think. I have done and will continue to train to do my best.

- The realization that I am prepared. I have done the training.

- An ironman is an ironman.

- I can overcome obstacles and have experienced pushing through, even if it didn't deliver the result I wanted, I still finished. I did what others have not been able to do.

- I really already am a champion. I have actually swum, biked and ran more than five times the distances required to be an ironman in my months of training. The only thing different is crossing the line that day.

- I will get the sleep I need before the races.

- I will be able to focus on nutrition to improve my performance more by not self-doubting myself with the swim, bike, and run portions.

We reframed John's activating event. Instead of I'm afraid of failing the Ironman, his new belief, which he wrote in the A2 column, was I do not have a fear of failing in the Ironman.

Then he wrote, Because...and followed that with his new beliefs about himself. Finally, he wrote his which makes me feel statements. Together, these statements combined to provide John with an affirmation that made him see himself in a very different light. I can't tell you how powerful this is!

So, how did this ultimately affect John's performance? He was able to complete his first full Ironman event. "John! You ARE an Ironman!" He put his new belief in place and acted upon it. His performance helped him to validate his new beliefs. John went on to complete another full Ironman event shortly thereafter, knocking well over an hour off his time.

This reminds me of Roger Bannister's story. He was the first person to complete a sub-four-minute mile run. At the time, no one thought a sub-four-minute mile run was possible—just as John felt it wasn't possible for him to complete a full Ironman. Shortly after Bannister hit a sub-four-minute mile, many other athletes ran sub-four-minute miles. And just like that, once John completed and actualized his first full Ironman, he absolutely killed his next Ironman. The power of the mind. The power of your beliefs.

A I am not a good runner.

B
1. I do not have a history or experience in running.
2. As much as I have improved on form I feel like I have more to work on.
3. I'm not as fast as I want to be.

C
1. I discredit myself because I think I need a certain amount of time or history to be taken seriously as a runner. I tell myself "I am not a runner" because I have not met some kind of standard or required time in the sport.
2. I do form checks as I run.
3. Knowing this is my greatest area for growth and potential, I'm impatient and hard on myself in building speed.

D
1. A year ago I could barely run 2 miles and I was in pain. Now... I run pain free, two miles is my warm up, and I have run a full marathon and a couple half marathons!
2. My run form has changed dramatically from my first track day! My form was good enough to get me through a full marathon AFTER a long swim and bike!
3. Speed means nothing if you cannot endure the distance. I can endure and not destroy myself in the process!

E
1. Where is the stupid list I feel I need to check off a certain amount of time or distance before I call myself a runner?!? Oh wait, there isn't one... Because I made it up! My accomplishments in just one short year, gives testament to my abilities because I DON'T have the history!
2. Reminder of how far I have come in such a short time.
3. Pushing my endurance is my goal and more important than my speed because without endurance speed does not exist.

DIAGRAM 9B - REAL-LIFE EXAMPLE OF IRRATIONAL BELIEFS AND THE ABCDE TECHNIQUE

Jennifer is another triathlete who can provide us with a real-life example of the ABCDE technique, shown in Diagram 9B, "Real-Life Example of Irrational Beliefs and the ABCDE Technique." She came to me with concerns that needed to be addressed.

Jennifer never felt like she was a good runner. After some conversation, I found that she was comparing herself to other runners. She looked at what her peers were doing and if she didn't measure up, she considered herself too slow.

Her activating event was, *I tell myself that I'm not a good runner.* Again, as her coach, I agreed with her.

Okay, so you're not a good runner, I said. *Why do you believe that you're not a good runner?*

Jennifer listed her beliefs:

- *I do not have a history or experience in running and as much as I've improved on form, I feel like I have more to work on.*

- *I am not as fast as I want to be.*

Fair enough. She didn't believe she was a good runner or fast enough. By the way, if these concerns seem trivial to you, that's a common assessment from someone who isn't dealing with the same challenges. A major obstacle to one person can seem unimportant to someone else. Likewise, many of the challenges that you deal with would probably seem trivial to another person. However, they're all truths to the person who's experiencing them, and debating is the key to uncovering their irrationality.

I asked Jennifer to describe the consequences of her beliefs to me, and she said the following:

- *I discredit myself because I think I need a longer race history to be taken seriously as a runner.*

- *I tell myself I am not a runner because I have not met some kind of standard or required time in the sport.*

Jennifer was judging herself solely on how long she'd been running. She went on to tell me about more consequences of her beliefs.

She said that she does form checks when she runs, constantly scanning her form to ensure she's moving properly. The problem with constant form checks is that—just like thinking about the mechanics of hitting a baseball—they slow you done.

People who've been runners for a while know their speed without thinking about it. They rely on their subconscious minds to drive their motor automation, and know their own bodies well enough to know their pace and how fast they're moving. However, by doing form checks, Jennifer engaged her prefrontal cortex, which took over in order to debate and discuss with the motor cortex everything her body was doing. Adding that in her pathway slowed her down.

Form checks are fine. Typically, runners do them quickly and keep moving. However, if you focus on them, they'll slow you down. One of the consequences of Jennifer's belief that she was slow and had bad running form was correcting the problem with so many form checks that she was slowing herself down.

Knowing that form and speed were her greatest areas for growth and potential, she was impatient and very hard on herself when results didn't come quickly enough.

In everything that we do, we need patience. In fact, you should be impatient to be patient. In anything you're attempting to accomplish, become patient as quickly as you can.

In physical challenges, the body has to go through processes to improve and that takes time and patience. If you're not patient, you'll become frustrated and you may just give up—or worse, end up hurting yourself.

I spoke to Jennifer and asked her to debate her beliefs. Was it true that she didn't have a history or experience in running?

She told me that a year ago she could barely run two miles and was in a lot of pain when she ran. Now, she said, she was running pain-free, two-mile warm-ups. She'd run a couple of half marathons and a full one. Talking about it, she realized that she did have a running history and was a pretty good runner. She'd made enormous improvements in a short time.

Jennifer debated her belief that she needed to work on her form. She realized that her form had improved dramatically since her first training day. She'd done a full Ironman, and her running form was good enough to carry her through it after a long swim and a bike ride.

Finally, Jennifer debated her belief that she wasn't as fast as she wanted to be. She realized that speed wasn't important if she didn't have the endurance to finish a long race, and that the faster she ran, the more her endurance would suffer. So, while some runners focus on how fast they are, Jennifer understood that she needed to stop worrying about it.

After debating each belief, Jennifer came to see herself as a good runner. She realized that she had become a runner the first time she ran, and had continued to be a runner for the past year. She had a running history and had made great strides in that year. Jennifer created an affirmation, her A2, and never looked back.

CHAPTER

MINDSET SHIFT TOOL 2: THE KICK-ASS YOU

In Chapter 6, you learned how to create new beliefs with the ABCDE technique. By identifying, questioning, and debunking your existing irrational beliefs and replacing them with rational, positive beliefs, you can rebuild the complex engine of your mind.

You can limit the development of *new* irrational beliefs by proactively managing your thoughts in real time. It starts with planting the right seeds.

PLANT THE RIGHT SEEDS

Think of your mind as a fertile garden and of thoughts

as seeds. A garden supports seeds and helps them grow. It provides the earth, nutrients, water, and sunshine the seeds need to flourish.

The garden doesn't care if the seeds grow into a tree that bears delicious, nutritious fruit, or sour, poisonous berries. Whatever grows from those seeds is predestined and there's nothing the garden can do to change that. It doesn't differentiate; it provides the same amount of resources to each seed that's planted.

Like the garden helps seeds grow, your mind helps your thoughts grow and it doesn't care if the thoughts are good or bad for you. That's why you have to be selective about the thoughts you plant. Whatever thoughts you entertain are going to grow, and grow, and grow, because your mind is going to give them everything they need to proliferate. You reap what you sow, good or bad.

If you plant positive thoughts, they'll blossom into wonderful experiences, and then you get to harvest the bounty of positive thoughts. However, if you plant negative thoughts, the garden of your mind bears bad experiences that sour your life like poison berries. You have a choice. You can sow good seeds or bad seeds.

Choosing good thoughts doesn't require you to be

oblivious to the bad ones. You know that negative thoughts are out there; however, you make the conscious choice to sow and nurture positive ones.

Acknowledge the bad thoughts. See them as opportunities for learning and growth. In this way, you strip them of their poison and they can't hurt you. Save your focus—the garden of your conscious mind—for positive thoughts that fill your life with the fruits of success.

To revisit the car analogy, let's say you need gas and as you drive down the road, you see a particular gas station that has been known to have water in their gas. Their gas prices are lower than anyone else's, though. Would you fill your tank up with that gas? Of course not. Even though it might save you some money, there is a strong chance the gas could cause engine problems. By the same token, if you fill your head with the most convenient thoughts—which are usually negative—your head is going to develop all kinds of knocks and pings. You don't want a noisy engine—you want a mindset that purrs like a kitten when you're at rest and roars like a lion when you hit the gas. You need good gas to do that. You need to fill up with positive thoughts.

CHOOSE THE RIGHT WORDS

As we discussed in Chapter 2, neuroplasticity allows your

CHANGE YOUR SELF-TALK, CHANGE YOUR THINKING

Have you ever been told to change your thinking? Did you know how? You will find this with many motivational speakers. "Change your thinking," they say; however, they don't tell you how. I would hypothesize that they don't actually know how to change your thinking. They're essentially echoing what others have said in the past. So, why? Thinking seems like something that isn't tangible, something you can't touch. While that's correct, it feels almost off-limits. I teach people how to change their thinking pretty quickly. How? Change your self-talk—that conversation in your head—and instantly, your thoughts change. Remember, your self-talk is your thought, is your focus, is your concentration, and is that which has your attention.

brain to evolve; however, unless you choose words that promote positive growth, your brain—and your mindset—won't develop in a way that delivers happiness. Thoughts, focus, self-talk, concentration, and attention are the same thing, and so when you control one of them, you control them all. *Self-talk*—the running conversation you have with yourself inside your head, your thoughts—is often negative and has a tendency to repeat itself. And as we discussed in Chapter 3, linguistics are a powerful force. Managing your self-talk is an important step toward controlling your focus and building a high performance mindset. Self-talk can either restrict or enhance the changes in your mindset that create your reality. So, how? Change your thoughts by changing your self-talk.

Words, phrases, and sentences comprise self-talk, and

so, you can begin to manage your self-talk by choosing language that works for you and eliminating language that works against you. Consider the following words and phrases:

- *I can't*, as in *I can't run that race, learn that new program,* or *have that kind of relationship.*
- *I'm never*, as in *I'm never going to be that fast, earn that much money,* or *be that happy.*
- *I could...but*, as in *I could compete in a triathlon, but I'm too slow (old, unprepared). I could get a better job, but I might not do well in a different position. I could ask that girl on a date, but she might turn me down.*
- *I'll try*, as in *I'll try to prepare for that race, look for a better job,* or *get a date.*

Can't. Never. Could...but. Try. Try? Why *try*? Why not *do*?

These are powerful words—powerfully *destructive* words—that inhibit your ability to perform, execute, create, act, and engage. When you choose to use these words, you're not choosing what you want. You're choosing what you don't want. When you choose what you don't want, that's exactly what you get.

Think about how these words make you feel when other people say them. Do they inspire confidence?

Let's say, for example, that you've been out of town all week and you're boarding a plane to come home. It's five o'clock and your ride home from the airport is caught up doing something else they can't pull away from. You think for a minute and know that I'm usually around, so you call me.

Hey, Craig! I'm flying in at nine, and unfortunately, my ride canceled. I know this is last minute, however, I seriously need your help. I called you because you're so reliable. Would you mind picking me up from the airport tonight at nine? I would owe you big time!

Sure, I'll try!

What? Do you believe I'm going to show up? I mean, I might. I might not. You see, *try* has no commitment. I might show up, however, subconsciously, I might be saying "I'll try" because I feel there's a chance that I won't make it. That's what *try* usually means. It means that I'm not committed. So now, think about all the times you use *try* knowing that you're not committed. *Try* is not an actionable word.

The minute you say or think *can't, never, could...but,* or *try,* you stop yourself from acting. Although you may not realize you're doing this, and you may actually think you might act, the fact is that once you've put those words into your head, your subconscious mind gloms onto them and applies those words to every conscious thought you have about whatever you want to do, have, or make. Negative words and phrases worm their way into your subconscious mind and sabotage your possibilities.

Failure is another word you should banish from your vocabulary. Interestingly enough, people fear failure because it has the potential to affect their identity. When you fail, you become...a failure! No one wants to be a failure so let's not even take that risk! *Wait just one minute.* What about all those books? *Fail your way to success,* they say. *Failure is the only way.* Does that even make sense? In fact, that sounds downright painful. If I have to fail to succeed, umm...NO!

Allow me to explain. Let's say you're driving down the road and your engine light comes on. Your car starts acting funny and begins to lose power. You pull over on the side of the road and call your mechanic friend. He comes to check out your car, and he tells you that you've experienced engine failure. What does this mean? It means the engine quit. So, engine failure equates to the engine quitting. This means that failure is to quit. However, as long as you're continuing to create action, learning from the results and applying that new learning to more action, you can never fail. It's just not possible.

Negative words—like *try, can't, never, could...but*, and my all-time favorite, *failure*—you use within your self-talk to deliver an unhappy reality. Self-talk can also promote wonderful, amazing, positive growth in your brain. It can do that with affirmations.

THE POWER OF AFFIRMATIONS

Affirmations are a specific kind of self-talk and a critical tool for developing a high performance mindset. Some claim affirmations do not work due to an assumed lack of empirical evidence; however, that's not true. Empirical evidence now supports affirmations. Current research finds that self-affirmation results in an increase in positive self-image when used by individuals who are confident in themselves and by individuals who have low self-esteem.

Consider the fact that 80 percent of your thoughts—and so 80 percent of your self-talk—is negative. Can you imagine if you spoke to your friends and your family the same way you speak to yourself? If you did, they wouldn't like you anymore!

You care about your friends and you wouldn't say negative things to them 80 percent of the time. In fact, if you talk to your friends like you talk to yourself, you are going to have zero friends! So why do you waste most of your self-talk repeating bad things to yourself? You must be your number one fan before anyone else will be your fan!

I AM NOT

- I am not confident.
- I am not enough.
- I am not good where I am.
- I am not attractive.
- I am not strong.
- I am not worthy of love.
- I am not happy.
- I am not courageous.
- I am not creative.
- I am not a champion.
- I am not a winner.
- I am not a badass.

I AM

- I am a good person.
- I am a good son/daughter.
- I am a good boyfriend/girlfriend.
- I am passionate.
- I am loving.
- I am caring.
- I am committed.
- I am loyal.
- I am honest.

- I am confident.
- I am enough.
- I am good where I am.
- I am attractive.
- I am strong.
- I am worthy of love.
- I am happy.
- I am courageous.
- I am creative.
- I am a champion.
- I am a winner.
- I am a badass.

DIAGRAM 10 - AFFIRMATION

It's time to change the script. Take a look at Diagram 10, "Affirmations." This is an example of an exercise you can do right now to help you change your script.

///

EXERCISE 4: AFFIRMATIONS

STEP ONE

Take a piece of paper and draw a line down the middle. On the left side of the paper, write down all the things you believe you are *not*, every positive quality that you believe you're lacking. Strangely enough, it's much easier for most people to write down what they *aren't* than to write down what they *are*. Remember, we have a negative bias by default. Each sentence should begin with, *I am not*. Dig deep! For example, *I am not successful, I am not wealthy, I am not attractive,* and *I am not happy*. Be honest with yourself and know that it's okay to document these feelings and beliefs about yourself. No one else is ever going to see this paper unless you share it.

STEP TWO

On the right side of the paper, write down everything you are—all of your positive qualities. Each statement should begin with the words, *I am*. Dig deep here, too. This isn't the time to be humble! You have many positive qualities and it's okay to feel good about yourself. Society gives us the impression that this can be interpreted as arrogance. It's important to understand that arrogance is not a sign of overconfidence, it's a sign of a lack of confidence. If a person acts big and strong, no one will question their lack of confidence, or so they think. Seriously, if this makes you uncomfortable, that's all the more reason to complete this powerful exercise. If you're having trouble coming up with a list, ask yourself questions like:

- Am I a good person?
- Am I a good son or daughter?
- Am I a good mother or father?
- Am I a good sister or brother?
- Am I a good friend?
- Am I loving, compassionate, loyal, or honest?
- Am I a champion?
- Am I a badass?

Those are all good qualities that probably describe you. Write them down. For some people, this exercise is easier if you do it with someone you trust. If you need help, have a friend ask you questions about yourself, and then ask them the same questions. You can build your lists together. Either way, if you feel a little uncomfortable doing this, that's normal. Your discomfort exists because you're used to focusing on what you perceive to be your shortcomings and aren't used to focusing on your good qualities. You can change that with this exercise.

STEP THREE

Go back to the left side of the paper. You're now going to rewrite all of the *I am not* statements on the right side of your paper and turn them into *I am* statements. Add them to the bottom of the list on the right side of the paper. *I am not successful* becomes *I am successful*. *I am not organized* becomes *I am organized*.

I know you're going to say, "Craig, I know I'm not those things, though." This is the very reason you need to change them. As we talked about in Chapter 5, your subconscious is a recorder that is constantly listening to your verbal and nonverbal self-talk. You're so accustomed to saying *I am not* that saying *I am* feels weird. This is exactly why you need to do it.

STEP FOUR

Once you have transferred the left side to the right side, tear off the left side of the paper—all those irrational *I am not* statements. Shred it. Burn it. Get rid of that list of old, outdated, negative beliefs. Remember how we did this in

Chapter 6 as a symbolic gesture? From this point for
they don't exist anymore—not for you.

The right side of the paper is your new script. Each *I am*
statement is an affirmation that you can use to reprogram
your subconscious mind and change your mindset through
verbalization. Tape that piece of paper to your bathroom
mirror. Read it out loud every morning and every night.
Take it to work with you, along with your ABCDE exercise,
and find a place to read it at lunch. Look yourself in the
eyes and say each affirmation out loud, with intention.
Mean it and believe it.

★ ★ ★

This exercise seems so simple that most people who read
this won't believe that it even works. They'll doubt its
effectiveness and won't do it. They'll allow themselves
to believe that it doesn't work. What I can tell you is that
my clients bear witness to the power of this mindset shift
tool! Because you're reading this, I know you're not one of
the doubters. Promise me that you will do this. Actually,
do it right now. Then read it every day—morning, noon,
and night—for the next week. You'll be amazed at how
powerful this simple exercise can be for changing your

self-talk and the way you approach life. Changing your self-talk with affirmations will replace your irrational, negative thoughts over time and will change your reality. By later today, you're going to feel differently about yourself, and after a week, you'll be shocked that you didn't do this sooner. Affirmations are the key to uncovering your confidence and that newly found confidence will dramatically affect every conscious thought process. It will change your script and your mindset and point you in the direction of those things you want in life.

I was working with a client one day who was really down on himself. A long relationship he was involved in had just dissolved. He had a lot of self-doubt and couldn't see past the belief, "I'm not good enough." I gave him the ABCDE exercise and the affirmation exercise to complete. The next time I saw him, he didn't look any different. I knew immediately he hadn't completed the exercises I had given him. When we spoke, he was still down, so I looked at him and said, "Did you do the exercises?" I already knew the answer and before he could respond, I said, "No, you didn't! I already know." I said, "Life has a 98/2 rule. Ninety-eight percent of people will not do what it takes to be happier; however, two percent will. Those are the people who create action and absolutely kill it." His body started to convulse a bit as he said, "I'll do it right now!" He completed the exercises and set fire to the old beliefs. Then, I had him go into the bathroom and say his new beliefs and affirmations to himself in the mirror and out loud. He was a little shy at first, however, he went into the bathroom and verbalized them. Not five minutes later, he came out pointing to the "I AM" statements he created. "I AM all of this!" he said, "So heck with her; if she doesn't see it, I'll find someone who does!"

It only works if you do it. So, go and do it!

GIVE YOURSELF CREDIT

You're planting good seeds, eliminating negative self-talk and adding a lot of positive affirmations to those daily conversations you have with yourself. It's natural at this point for some people to start feeling a little regret over the fact that they didn't start this process sooner. Of course, you can replace that regret with reflection. You can choose to view your past experiences as opportunities for learning and in that way, create positive thoughts. You can also give yourself tremendous credit for your past experiences.

Get out your notebook. It's time to do some more writing.

EXERCISE 5: YOU'RE A BADASS!

STEP ONE

Write down every single bad experience you've ever had, all the horrible things that have happened to you and the horrible things you've done. Write them down as far back as you can remember so you can get all of them.

- Maybe you were assaulted when you were a kid.
- Maybe your parents beat you or you were bullied in school.
- Maybe you wrecked your dad's car.
- Maybe you got fired from a job.

All that stuff is still in your head, like a big landfill stuffed with the garbage of your life. It stinks up there! Get it all out on the page. Get it out and give it some air.

You might need hours or even days to write everything down. Whew, this might be quite the undertaking; however, it is *soooo* worth it!

STEP TWO

When you're done, read it. Although it may be tough to

read, it's your life and no matter how bad it is or how ugly it got, it's yours—and it's okay. Everything about you—your past, present, and your future—is okay. You wouldn't be the person you are today without everything that has happened to you thus far. Remember that!

So, you read all of it. Wow, all of that has happened to you! And guess what? You're still here! You survived. Everything that has been thrown at you your whole life hasn't taken you down. You must be some kind of major badass to have gone through all those experiences and lived to tell the tale. You are tough. You are resilient. You're a survivor.

You may want to throw that piece of paper into the shredder or the fireplace; however, think about what all those things you wrote mean. Those experiences represent your life's most difficult challenges and if they didn't exist, you wouldn't be the person you are today. Acknowledge the hardest parts of your life and take credit for your resilience. You are you—the kick-ass you—because of what you've been through. Don't be ashamed of that. Own your scars and your survival. Wear that grit like a badge of honor. Instead of throwing this paper away, keep it and write at the bottom, "I am Resilient! I am Awesome! I am Unstoppable!" Just sit back and think about that for a minute. Consume the strength you have within you that has been awakened and acknowledge it! Keep this close so you can pull it out as a reminder when you get a little down.

★ ★ ★

Some people would like to erase their pasts; however, your life's experiences have extraordinary value. This is your path, and this is how you got here. Take credit for your life—every bit of it—and use it to your advantage. You can even choose to be grateful for your past. Seriously! Without it, you wouldn't be you and that would be sad. Use your past to reinforce what you're beginning to understand about yourself: You are pretty incredible! I am proud of you!

SELF-ACCEPTANCE

After you've given yourself credit for surviving all the past hardships of your life, take a moment to accept you for you. You are the culmination of all your experiences, both good and bad. Until you accept yourself for who you are, no one else will. Although your choices may have made life tough for you, the challenges you faced made you stronger. That drive inside of you, that determination and dedication you depend on to persevere and thrive—that comes from having to overcome challenges that tested you in your past. If everyone were to be the person you wanted them to be and if your path were easier, it would change everything about you. I'm pretty sure you'd rather be the badass you are right now!

You made a lot of decisions in your lifetime. Those decisions paved the path you took in life and brought you to where you are now. You may not like some of your past decisions; however, you can reflect on them and use your experience to plan for better decisions and happier outcomes in the future. Right now, though, accept where you are. Accept who you are. BREATHE! Accept all the choices you've made thus far. Those choices brought you here, to this place at this moment in your life. Accept yourself, knowing that from this point forward, you can make any choices you like. If you choose to adopt the techniques in this book, you'll develop a more positive attitude, enjoy more pleasant emotional and physiological responses, and take actions that direct you to a life where you get more of what you want.

CONFIDENCE

I'll tell you a secret: Everyone has confidence. Some people have just misplaced it. You absolutely have confidence, and I will tell you how to uncover it.

Confidence never leaves you, because it comes from

within. If you're looking outside yourself for confidence, you'll never find it. Confidence doesn't come from anywhere else—it comes from you. You can't buy a fast car and call it confidence. You can't pick up a box of confidence from Amazon Prime. You can't get a hot girlfriend or boyfriend and call that confidence, either. That's a phony kind of confidence and if you depend on external factors for confidence, it's not real, and it will not last!

External confidence can be taken away. For example, your car could be repossessed and your girlfriend could break up with you. Where's your confidence now? It's in the used car lot or on a date with another person. Lucky for you that wasn't real confidence anyway. You win your age group in an Ironman event. You get super confident! At your next Ironman race, you don't place in the top ten, so now where's your confidence? Yep, tanked!

Real confidence comes from within you, and you exude that confidence with your thoughts, your eyes, your posture, your body language, your words, and your actions. The more confident you are in how you manage those things, the more your confidence will build. You'll feel it, and all you have to do is practice. Use your confidence and it will grow.

Do you know someone who's lost their confidence? They

have trouble making eye contact. Their bodies sag and when you talk to them, they don't engage. They turn away as if to say, "I have no confidence in who I am. I can't interact and be human with you." There's nothing wrong with that person except that they've lost their confidence. You can find your confidence and build it with practice.

You see, the number one reason people lose confidence in themselves is they shift their focus on what they don't have instead of focusing on and appreciating what they do have.

Use your body to show your confidence. Stand tall with your shoulders back and your head high. Walk with purpose. Face people and look them in the eye when you talk to them. Hold their gaze and don't look down or turn away. Stop looking at others and wishing you had what they had. You don't know their story or their life. It is not always as peachy as you believe it to be.

Are you sitting down? Sit up straight. Lift your chest and arch your back. Feel strong. Be empowered. Confidence comes from within and when you act confident, it will rise to the occasion and show itself to the world. Remember to recognize what you do have; be grateful for those things and your confidence will begin to rise.

Your confidence will empower you to make better choices

that reflect your authentic self and you'll be less likely to give in to societal pressure. For example, if you want to go to the gym on Thursday night and your friends want you to go out drinking, your confidence will give you the power to make the choice that's best for you—not for them.

Confidence is life-changing and it's another tool that you already have. Find it, use it, and enjoy what happens.

WHAT DO I DO NEXT?

Let's be honest here. Changing your brain isn't rocket science—or brain surgery. Just follow the techniques in this book. So why isn't everyone walking around with a high performance mindset?

You have to act. You can't just read this book and expect a miracle. Nothing happens unless you choose to do the work. I can give you every mindset shift tool in my toolkit; however, if you don't use them, they certainly will not work. You have to use the ABCDE technique over and over again until it becomes part of your mindset. Don't just use it once; use it every time you have an issue, until you create a habit of using the tool and find yourself doing it automatically. You have to change that inner dialog you have with yourself—your self-talk—and fill it with affirmations day in and day out until you believe them. You have to own your past and take credit for it, too.

If you don't use any of these techniques, your life won't change. Some people who read this book won't use these techniques, or they'll use them once and then never use them again. That won't work. You have to use them and keep using them to get the results you want and the life you deserve. This isn't a "get a high performance mindset quick" scheme. Even though this is going to take work, wouldn't you say your life is worth it?

You bought this book to learn how to develop a high performance mindset and be more successful in business, sports, and life. That must mean something to you, so why give up so easily? The exercises are simple and take very little time. If you truly want to initiate dramatic changes in the way you think, and if you want to manifest a different life for yourself, realize that it is within your power. Of course, whether or not you choose to wield that power is up to you.

Change is going to happen anyway, whether you initiate it or not. Time passes and nothing is static. You can choose positive change or accept whatever change comes your way. The world doesn't happen to you, it happens for you. It's up to you to see it for what it is—a world of opportunities with the potential to give you everything you want.

All you have to do is act. All you have to do is ask for it—or rather, tell yourself to go and get it.

CHAPTER 08

MINDSET SHIFT TOOL 3: OWN YOUR FOCUS

The ABCDE technique and affirmations are techniques that change your subconscious mind by replacing old, negative beliefs with new, positive ones. Over time, regular application of these tools will change what you believe about yourself, which will then influence your conscious thoughts. Remember that your mindset is a combination of your subconscious mind and your conscious mind. In addition to altering your conscious thoughts, you can take control of them directly by owning your focus.

Your focus is whatever you're thinking about at the moment. Some people will tell you that you have multiple focuses; that's just not possible. Your focus is your thought, and you can only have one of them at a time. You can shift quickly back and forth between thoughts; however, you're still only having one at a time. Remember, it's the self-talk you're having with yourself, and you're giving it all your attention and concentration. Your focus, remember, drives your life's trajectory. If you think of your subconscious mind as a GPS filled with thousands of maps, imagine your conscious mind as the steering wheel.

Taking control of the 12,000–50,000 thoughts you have each day—the objects of your focus, self-talk, concentration, and attention—is like taking the wheel and driving your mindset, your thoughts, and your life in whatever direction you choose.

DRIVE YOUR FOCUS

Think of your life as a car and your focus as the steering wheel. When you turn the wheel to the right, your self-talk, concentration, and attention go in that direction. Your life goes in that direction, too. When you drive a car, you always have your hands on the wheel. You never let go of the wheel. You're always steering the car. It's the same with your focus. You're always focused.

Your mind doesn't just stop thinking. It's always focused on something. When people say they have trouble focusing, what they really mean is that they have trouble focusing on one thing for an extended period of time. While their focus is always shifting, there is always a focus.

When you're constantly turning the steering wheel on your car back and forth, you can end up going in circles. It's the same with your focus. If you want to get somewhere, you have to learn how to focus on one thing and go in one direction for as long as you need to.

Focus isn't taught directly at home or at school. Your teacher probably never said, "Today, kids, we're going to learn how to focus." However, your mom and dad may have inadvertently helped train your mind to focus when they read books to you or taught you how to tie your shoes or ride a bike. Your teachers may have helped you indirectly learn how to focus when they showed you how to solve math problems.

Someone taught you how to drive a car, probably one of your parents. When they took you out on the road, did they bring something for you to eat in the car? Did they invite grandma and grandpa along to chat with you while you were driving or tell you to bring your cell phone so you could text your friends while you were driving? No, they removed all those distractions, because they wanted you to focus on one thing—driving.

You had to focus when you were learning how to drive. In order to maintain and improve your power of focus, you have to continue training your mind. Not many people practice focusing techniques. This is why people get so distracted. You can increase your ability to focus by practicing techniques that force you to focus for a specific duration of time.

Learning to focus isn't always easy, because there are a lot of distractions vying for your attention. You have to train your mind to ignore them and concentrate on the thoughts you choose.

Consider all the distractions—all that stimuli—your mind has to deal with every day. Advertisers grab your attention all the time. Surf the internet and pay attention to all the sponsored ads with waving hands and the "news" articles with splashy images and catchy titles aimed at getting your attention. That "click-bait" hacks your concentration, lures you in, and steals your focus and your time. Whoever creates that stuff wants to sell you something, and the first step is getting your attention. You may not have logged on to your computer with the intention of buying something from one of these companies, yet you are willingly allowing them to steal your focus, your time, and—if you do end up buying from them—your money.

Focus on this little nugget of truth: Once something steals your time, you can never get it back. It's gone. Your most precious, limited resource—time—has just been hijacked.

Does your phone ding every time you get a new email or a social media notification? What does that do to your focus? Cell phones can be a huge distraction. Be aware of the stimuli in your surroundings that distract you and hijack your focus. Once you recognize these distractions, you can do something about them. Here's a better question: Why is it that you choose to pick up a ringing phone? You might say, "Because it's ringing," or "Someone might need me;" however, the truth is you picked up the ringing phone because you decided to. Your choice of focus is a decision that you make.

When you were learning how to drive, you had to focus on the road. With that said, that doesn't mean you ignored everything else. You had to be aware of other cars on the road, your speed, the road conditions, the directions you were taking, and pedestrians and bikers alongside the road and on the crosswalks. However, you made choices about your focus. You didn't stare out the windshield at the birds in the sky. You made decisions about what you let in and what you ignored, and you can learn to develop that same intentional focus in your life.

Learning how to control your focus and give your attention to one thing for an extended period of time takes practice. Once you learn how to control your focus, you will have better control over the direction of your life.

You can hang out in the backseat and go wherever life takes you, or you can get in the driver's seat and take the wheel. I'll ride shotgun, okay? Let's go for a spin.

FROM NINETY TO ZERO

There are a lot of distractions in your outside surroundings and many thoughts connected to the past, present, and future to choose from inside your head. That's why people have trouble focusing. With practice, you can select the thought you want to concentrate on and hang onto it for as long as you like.

EXERCISE 6: COUNTING BACKWARDS

STEP ONE

For this exercise, go to a quiet room. Take this book with you along with your pen and notebook, and leave your phone behind. If you have family or roommates, let them know that you need about thirty minutes of time alone, so they don't knock on the door or walk in on you. If it's still noisy in your house, put on some noise-canceling headphones.

Remove all distractions from the room, especially any electronic devices, like a laptop or a tablet. Get comfortable in that room.

STEP TWO

Now, close your eyes and count backwards from ninety to zero by threes. Counting backwards by threes isn't automatic and takes concentration, so you'll have to think about it. It will take all your focus. Say the numbers to yourself, using your self-talk to count: Ninety. Eighty-seven. Eighty-four. Eighty-one. Seventy-eight. Seventy-five, and so on.

Keep counting backward until you get distracted. At some point, you might realize you're hungry or tired or a random thought will wander into your head, and you'll stop counting and focus on that other thought. When that happens, open your eyes. Did you get to seventy-five? Did you make it all the way to zero? Write down the last number you counted before you were distracted.

Close your eyes and do it again. Keep practicing until you can get from ninety to zero without being distracted. Once you do that, count forward in threes, from zero to ninety.

Do it several times. If it becomes too easy, count from eighty to zero backward by fours, and then from zero to eighty by fours.

★ ★ ★

This is the way I help train my athletes to control their focus. When you focus on the numbers, you can't think about anything else. Practicing this way trains your mind to focus on one thing—counting numbers—and then you can use that focusing power to concentrate on other things whenever you need to.

After a while, you'll have the numbers memorized and counting them will be easy and automatic. When that happens, change the numbers to make it more difficult. Count backward from 210 to zero by sevens. Keep challenging yourself and your focus will improve. Soon enough, your active mind will stop driving around in circles. It will be parked in the garage and you'll be out—like the dashboard light. I will note that some people don't find numbers to be fascinating to work with. If this is the case, you could say

REAL-LIFE NINETY TO ZERO

Counting backwards trains your mind to control your focus, and it also works to help you fall asleep at night. If you have trouble clearing your mind of thoughts, count backward by threes, fours, sixes, sevens, eights, or nines. The exercise will take all your focus and you won't be able to think about anything else. In fact, one of my clients, professional triathlete Nickie Luse used this technique. Here's what she told me about it:

I was having trouble focusing and falling asleep at night as my mind would wander, especially in the bulk of my training and racing season. I laughed when Craig told me to count backward, but he assured me I wouldn't be able to think of anything else. The concentration it takes to count backward had me focusing on completing the task and it also calmed my mind as I couldn't let myself think of anything else without messing up my numbers game. I'm not sure I ever made it to zero before falling asleep. So, some people might count sheep, but counting numbers backward created a focus and eliminated any noise in my brain and helped me drift off to sleep.

—Nickie

It works for Nickie, who has a *lot* to think about the night before a race! It will work for you, too.

Or, how about elite triathlete Mike Kloosterman? He utilized the same technique to help him achieve a personal best swim. Here's what Mike had to say:

Counting backward... No way something that simple can work... How many things can the mind truly focus on at any given time?

One.

For me, it was panic attacks and deeply rooted anxiety during the swim leg of any triathlon. It had gotten to the point where I just accepted the inevitable and waited for the fear to wash over and physically stop me in my tracks. Once it took hold I could finally settle down, let everyone pass, and then mope my way to the end of the swim. People said I went out too hard initially, or I was being overly aware of my surroundings and I just needed to ignore the feeling altogether and muscle through it. But it was more than that. I felt out of control in a bad way. The world was shrinking in. All of the hard work of training and preparation, poof, squandered in the first three minutes of the event.

Key word there, WAS.

By simply counting backward I was able to effectively block out the majority of stimuli that put me in overload. At first, I couldn't even make it from one hundred down to ninety-two. However, I kept at it and each time I lost track I'd start again; one hundred, ninety-nine, ninety-eight, ninety-seven, ninety-six... It took several attempts to even make it past 50 but sure enough once I really truly focused on simply counting backwards I made it to zero...twice. The result? A personal best swim in a Full Distance IRONMAN with a mass start nonetheless.

—Mike Kloosterman

When we have what we feel are big issues, we often overlook simple fixes because we feel our big issues need a big fix. Mike proved that to be wrong.

the alphabet backwards, using every other letter. While this is more challenging, it uses the same methodology.

OBJECT IDENTIFICATION

This exercise is a little more difficult; however, you're learning fast and you can do this. You'll need a timer, your notebook, and a pen. You can set a timer on your cell phone, watch, or laptop.

EXERCISE 7: OBJECT IDENTIFICATION

STEP ONE

Get an object from around your house that you can hold in

your hand. Anything will do—a can of food, a package, a picture, or anything else you have handy. For this example, we'll use an empty soda can.

STEP TWO

Start the timer. Hold the can in front of your face and describe it. Give that soda can your full attention and describe every detail out loud. You might say something like this: "It's shaped like a cylinder and it's about six or eight inches tall and maybe three inches across the top. It's light because it's empty, and it's made of something shiny, probably aluminum."

Describe the label and read the ingredients. Keep talking about that can until another thought distracts you—a thought that has nothing to do with the can. Stop the timer and write down how many seconds you focused on the can before you were distracted.

STEP THREE

Now, challenge yourself. Restart the timer and do it again. Then do it again. Keep doing it and keep writing down the time. You should be able to focus on that can for increasingly longer periods of time. You're learning how to pay attention to the can and talk about it, and something else is happening, too. You're training your mind to focus on something—one thing—for an extended period of time. Now you can use that power of concentration to focus in a race, a presentation at work, or a task you need to complete. The can is practice for focusing on what's important to you in life.

★ ★ ★

Once you're comfortable with these concentration techniques, challenge yourself by adding a distraction. Leave your phone or your laptop on during the counting exercise or the object identification exercise. Your phone will buzz and beep, and your laptop will beg for your attention. Ignore them. Maintain your focus. Just as you made a habit of immediately attending to your phone, you can make a habit of waiting until you are done with your focus exercises before checking it.

Both of these techniques work by intentionally attaching your focus to something—numbers or an object—for a period of time without being distracted. By intentionally maintaining your focus on the selected activity or object, you have control of the wheel and can guide your thoughts in any direction you please. Instead of being a passenger along for the ride, you're in the driver's seat.

The key to their effectiveness is making sure they're difficult enough to force you to concentrate, while not so difficult that you give up easily or get distracted by another thought. That's why you have to count backward by a number that doesn't follow an obvious pattern. Counting backward by ones, twos, fives or tens, for example, would be too easy and your mind would wander.

Do these exercises every day. Think of them as push-ups for your brain. Each day, add another distraction. Keep challenging your power of concentration. Over time, you'll be amazed at how many distractions you can ignore.

Learning to control your focus is one of the most important skills you can master. Until you learn how to do it at-will, you'll constantly be distracted by what other people want you to focus on. Keep practicing until you own your focus.

MINDFULNESS AND MEDITATION

You've probably heard of mindfulness and meditation. For many people, using mindfulness and meditation is mysterious. Some have even expressed a bit of fear because of their lack of knowledge about either. Remember, fear often stems from a lack of knowledge. In fact, I've had conversations with mindfulness and meditation coaches who, when asked, admitted to me that they didn't truly understand HOW either one of them works. Here's what I want you to know about both: The fundamental reason they work to reduce your anxiety and depression is that they hack the three references of time I discussed in Chapter 4. When you're mindful of your present thoughts or when you're using breathing meditation, both are "present moment" activities. If you'll recall, you can only have one thought at a time, and it will either be a future thought, a present thought, or a past thought. You cannot have a thought that's in more than one reference of time. Thus, when you focus on a present moment activity, you can't be depressed or anxious. That's it—nothing more, nothing less. So, if you haven't taken a class in mindfulness or meditation—or learned about them on your own by reading a book—you should consider it.

Mindfulness and meditation will help you be present and will be a great addition to the tools in this book, especially now that you know what's happening behind the scenes. They're convenient techniques because they're free and you can practice them anywhere. There's no gear, or anything else—except your mind—required. You can practice these techniques on anything; however, the most common object is breathing. Wherever you go and whatever you're doing, you always have your breath. It's continuous and it's always in the present moment. As long as you're alive, you're breathing.

EXERCISE 8: FOCUS ON YOUR BREATH

When you focus your mind on your breath, you have to think in the present—you have to be mindful. You're not thinking about your past breath or your future breath. You're not feeling anxious or depressed. You're existing in the present moment and your only thought is breathing. Do it.

STEP ONE

Close your eyes and commit all your focus to breathing. Breathe in and breathe out. Feel your lungs fill up with air as you inhale, and feel the air rush from your lungs as you exhale.

STEP TWO

Imagine your breath is a color. What color is the air you breathe in and what color is the air you breathe out? Make it any color you like. Feel your chest rise and fall, rise and fall, and see the colors swirling as the air enters and leaves your body.

Focusing all your attention on those breaths is mindful meditation. There's nothing mystical or weird about it. It's another very effective technique for training your mind to focus with a present-moment activity.

★ ★ ★

Now you have three techniques to develop your ability to focus. Use them. Practice at least one of these techniques every day and your powers of concentration will improve. Develop your ability to focus and take control of your conscious mind. By controlling your conscious mind, you can reprogram your subconscious mind and then you'll have a more rational, positive filter through which to experience the world. You'll move forward, progressing in the direction you want to go and getting what you want in life.

Everything in this world that you get or do not get depends on your focus; so, the more skilled you become at owning your focus, the more control you'll have over your results, your outcomes, your life, and your future.

CHAPTER

MINDSET SHIFT TOOL 4: VISUALIZE YOURSELF TO A HIGH PERFORMANCE MINDSET

You just completed exercises that help you improve your focus control. Now it's time for more fun.

Visualization is the process of imagination. It's seeing a picture or a movie inside your head and experiencing that movie with all your senses.

Remember that your subconscious mind doesn't know the difference between visualization—whatever you imagine—and reality. In other words, if you visualize running, the same parts of your brain used to run will engage while you visualize.

Visualization is also useful whenever you want to create calm in your life. Maybe you had a hectic day and you want to unwind. Instead of reaching for a beer or turning on the television, visualize a relaxing experience.

You can visualize by reflecting on a pleasant activity from your past and "reliving" it in your imagination, or you can create a new experience in your mind that you make up.

EXERCISE 9: VISUALIZATION

STEP ONE

For this exercise, think about a pleasant experience you've had. Did you go to the beach last weekend? If not, let's act as if you did. Get comfortable, close your eyes, and visualize what it was like at the beach. Imagine the warm sun on your skin and the sand between your toes. The sound of the waves is soothing and there's a gentle breeze. You have a cold drink in your hand. Smell the coconut. Taste the pineapple.

If you prefer, you can reflect on another memory or make something up. Your visualizations are all your own and they can be about anything that makes you happy. Just like counting and object identification, visualization is a controlled method of focusing your thoughts on something that you choose to think about.

STEP TWO

Visualization is also a great technique for preparing for a big event like a race, a meeting, or a goal you want to accomplish. By visualizing the event before it happens, you'll prepare your mind for it and lessen any anxiety you might be feeling.

For example, say you have a big race coming up. You're competing in a triathlon. You need to get a lot of sleep; however, your pre-race anxiety is going to keep you awake. While you could go back and use the ABCDE technique in Chapter 6, you can also use visualization to get some sleep and help your mind prepare for the race.

First, research tells us not to worry about sleeping the night before the event. How much sleep you get the night before a race or event has a trivial effect on the final outcome compared to the rest you've been getting leading up to the race. If you've been training, eating right, and allowing your body to recover for months, one night with little sleep won't make much difference in how you perform. Interestingly enough, when I tell my athletes this, they immediately feel relieved. So, don't worry if you don't get much sleep.

The night before the race, as you are getting into bed and getting comfortable, lie down in bed, pull the covers up, and close your eyes. I want you to start visualizing the next day—race day.

Pretend it's 3:30 in the morning, or whatever time you're going to get up. Visualize getting up after a good night's sleep. Imagine yourself stretching and feeling refreshed and energized. In your mind's eye, brush your teeth, get cleaned up, and enjoy your delicious pre-race breakfast. Get all your things together that you're bringing with you to the race. You probably have them packed already. Think about each item. Visualize going to the race, dropping off your gear at the transition, and getting in line to start your swim.

Use all your senses to imagine the cool, crisp air and the smells of the water. You can hear a lot of chattering and laughter. People are happy to be at the triathlon, competing alongside you.

You hear the shot and the music. As you make your way

to the edge of the water, you jump in. Start swimming. Imagine what it feels like to swim. You can feel your body glide through the water. You are excited for all the day has in store for you. This is what you have been waiting for.

If you're like most people, your visualization won't last to the transition, because you'll fall asleep before you even get in the water. Success! Now you're sleeping and your mind is ready for that race.

★ ★ ★

You can use this same technique to prepare for a speaking engagement. Don't worry about sleeping the night before your speech, just go to bed and visualize the next day. It's going to be a great day! Imagine it: You'll wake up excited about the speech. You'll shower, shave, and get dressed. People will be happy to see you, and you'll be on stage looking out at all their smiling faces. You're going to crush it.

Again, visualization used this way will help you fall asleep and will also prepare your mind for the next day's event. By visualizing the event as a positive experience, you'll remove a lot of the worry. Visualizing a race, a speaking presentation or a date that goes well prepares your mind for success. Remember that your subconscious mind doesn't know the difference between visualization and reality, so imagining a positive experience will put you in the right frame of mind for the occasion.

Visualization is effective the night before an important event, and you can continue to use it leading up to the event. If you're sitting in a restaurant waiting for your date to show up, visualize how the evening's going to go. Imagine your date walking into the restaurant and being thrilled—and maybe a little relieved—to see you sitting there, waiting for him or her. Your date is smiling from ear to ear. They pull up a seat at your table, take your hand, look you in the eyes, and lean in to tell you how wonderful it is to see you. It's going to be a great evening and your mind is all ready for it.

If you're waiting to give a presentation, find a quiet spot, close your eyes, and focus on your breathing with mindful meditation. Then imagine what it will be like to address the crowd. Visualize the audience smiling and clapping as you take the stage, laughing at your first joke, and listening intently as you mesmerize them with your speech. Imagine the roar of the crowd as you close your speech with something clever and inspirational. The audience is on its feet and everyone is cheering. People approach the stage to thank you and shake your hand. Some of them want your autograph and a "selfie" for their social media site. Feel the love of the crowd wash over you. Breathe, smile, and move. Your mind is ready for that presentation. You have the right mindset for it and the experience will be as successful and spectacular as you imagined.

VISUALIZING CHALLENGES AND ACHIEVEMENTS

Visualization can also be used when working toward a goal or preparing for a challenge.

Preparing for the future while being in the moment—which we discussed in Chapter 4—comes into play here, because you are visualizing the achievement of a goal before you achieve it. In this way, you prepare yourself for that moment in the future. You prepare your mind for that goal. The outcome of an event during visualization should be positive, even if you choose to visualize challenges. For example, if you're competing in an Ironman Triathlon, it's okay to visualize yourself getting a flat tire during the biking leg of the competition. In fact, imagining challenges like a flat tire can help your mind prepare to manage potential issues.

So, your bike gets a flat during the race. What do you do? Visualize yourself pulling off to the side of the road. You're calm because you knew this could happen and you're prepared to handle it. You don't rush because you know that's what leads people to make mistakes. You get out your tools and you fix the flat. Mentally walk through the process. Then get on your bike and get back in the race.

Visualizing challenges and the steps required to overcome them will prepare you for when they do happen. You'll also be less likely to stress out about the possibility of them happening, because you've thought it through and you know how you'll react.

If you're giving a speech, visualize yourself forgetting one of your lines or forgetting to make a particular point. What will happen? Nothing will happen because no one in the audience knows what you planned to say. Only you know that. Imagine how you'll handle it. Can you make the point later in the speech? Or should you skip it and continue on with the rest of your speech? Either way, visualizing that error and imagining how you'll handle it will lessen any stress you have about flubbing a speech, and if it does happen, you'll be prepared to handle it.

As you develop a high performance mindset, imagining challenges will become easier because you'll view obstacles as opportunities. Opportunities are your chance to learn something new. If you never get a flat tire during training, you'll never have the chance to learn how to fix or change one. If you never flub a speech, you'll never have the chance to learn how to recover. Each time you're challenged and you recover, your belief in your abilities will be reinforced.

You may not be in control of external factors—like a nail in the road or someone in the audience coughing or interrupting your speech—however, you are in control of how you manage those issues. You are in control of your thoughts and your actions, and that's what matters. That is your focus.

WHY VISUALIZATION WORKS

Visualization works for several reasons. First, your subconscious mind doesn't know the difference between what you imagine and what is real. It observes the stimuli and creates beliefs no matter where the images come from—the outside world or the world inside your head.

It also works because you can only focus on one thing at a time, so if you focus on a visualized scenario where you get to make all the decisions about how that scenario plays out, you can't focus on anything else. Your mind won't be overrun with stress-inducing distractions. Since visualization occurs in the present moment, it isn't plagued by depressive thoughts of the past or anxious thoughts about the future. Visualization is a positive experience in this perspective.

Visualization allows you to consider stressful events you would typically not want to think about, from a controlled, productive perspective. It's your own form of virtual reality. For example, if you're stressed about an upcoming date, you attempt to not think about it. The problem is, the more you attempt to not think about it, the more you do think about it, and not in a positive way. You think about it with anxiety instead of preparation. Giving yourself permission to think about a future event and visualize it decreases your anxiety and creates calm.

Imagining disastrous results will increase the likelihood of manifesting a disaster; however, if you allow yourself to imagine successful results—even if the success is fraught with challenges that you have to overcome—you will manifest a successful outcome.

Here's one last thought before we move on to Part III: The bottom line is that when you visualize, you choose to put positive thoughts in your head. Although it takes some work, the payoff is grand.

PART III

PUTTING IT ALL TOGETHER

CHAPTER

RELATIONSHIPS WITH OTHERS...AND YOURSELF

Developing a high performance mindset may seem like a solitary endeavor. However, success of any kind—in business, sports, and life—requires good relationships.

Without others, success is difficult (if not impossible) to achieve in any field. Although your knowledge is partly due to experience, much of what you know was passed down to you by parents, teachers, and mentors, and through books. For every scientist, engineer, doctor, business person, or athlete, there are many people who paved the way for their success. You can leverage the knowledge developed by others and build on it to achieve your own goals.

People are the common denominator in every career, and relationships matter in every industry. You may be in business, banking, or retail and think your focus is on profits, finance, and sales; however, your real job is interacting well with people. Some may help you—and you can accept their support—while others may present challenges, which you can use as opportunities for learning. When you focus on your relationships and your customers, the profits will come—not the other way around.

Positive relationships and the high performance mindset feed off each other. If you have one, you probably have the other as well. Difficult relationships can cause negativity and decrease your mental performance. They can affect you emotionally and physiologically, and be a distraction. That's the opposite of a high performance mindset. If you don't get along with other people, you'll have a tough time accomplishing anything in any career. With a high performance mindset, you exude positivity and confidence, attracting other like-minded people who want you to succeed.

Good relationships matter in sports, too. If you have a coach, team, or a training partner, those relationships will drive your success. You have seen bad team relationships; they never perform well.

Finally, good relationships at home with your family are critical for developing a healthy mindset. Your family life affects every other part of your life. When you're having struggles at home, you can't forget about them when you go to work or go out for a run. They're always there in your mind and you have to deal with them. Strong relationships with the people you care about make developing a positive, high performance mindset more achievable.

THE LAW OF ATTRACTION

Like minds are attracted to each other, so if you have a positive mindset you'll attract other positive people. The same holds true for negative mindsets. However, if you attempt to stay away from certain people, you'll attract them in handfuls. Whatever (and whomever) you focus your attention on, you attract—both good and bad.

Let's be honest with each other, holding onto negative relationships with people who wear you down doesn't leave much room for positive relationships with people who energize you. It's hard to let go of people, I get that; however, if people in your personal or professional life are affecting your ability to focus on getting what you want in life, you have to consider limiting your time with them or letting go of them altogether.

While that may sound harsh, surrounding yourself with negative people is settling for less than you deserve. You have to be willing to leave relationships that aren't helping you to make room for better ones. Letting go of the bad also opens the door for helping others. You must give first to receive.

CHOOSE YOUR FRIENDS WISELY

Cultivating new relationships with people who lift you up is important because over time, you become more and more like your closest friends. While that's great if you and your friends have similar goals, it won't work out for you if their goals contradict yours.

For example, if you want to run marathons and your friends party hard, you'll be more likely to stay up late, have a poor diet, and skip training. Oh, that peer pressure. If you're generally engaged at work and always challenging yourself to learn new skills, and your coworkers are always complaining about how much they hate the job, you'll be less likely to move up. It's too easy to get pulled into a negative mindset when you're surrounded by people who think negatively.

Have you ever heard a person at work complain about something, for example, their child's teacher? Did anyone respond by coming to the defense of teachers? Maybe—not likely. They all jumped on the bandwagon and probably even complained about their own kids' teachers. You may have even added your own two cents to the conversation. The funny thing is, your child may have a wonderful teacher. However, the conversation isn't about what everyone likes about teachers, it's about what everyone doesn't like. It's much easier to agree with everyone—and offer your own story about some god-awful thing your child's teacher did that one time.

So now your focus is on the negative. It shifts to the negative whenever you're around people who are negative. The more time you spend around people like that, the more comfortable you'll become around them—and it's hard to get out of that rut. If this is you, make the decision to get out of that pothole. Vow to find new people to hang out with who can improve your mindset and your life instead of pulling you down with them.

ROMANTIC RELATIONSHIPS VERSUS FRIENDSHIPS

The same principles that govern your friend choices should also be applied to choosing your romantic partners. Before you get involved with someone, ask yourself if they're the kind of person you should be around.

There's a strange notion that people are either in the "friend zone" or they're potential—or actual—partners; however, anyone you spend a lot of time with should be a friend. Look at all the people in your life as friends, first. A strong foundation of friendship provides a solid platform for more intimate relationships that may develop over time.

It's a common misconception that once someone is a friend, they're automatically designated to the "friend zone" and thus, undateable. The truth is, you're better off developing a friendship with a person first and then deciding if you want to take the relationship further. So, bottom line: Your friends are dateable. Although you may not *want* to date them, friends and partners aren't mutually exclusive groups.

Again, the same principles that govern your friendships should govern your choice of romantic partners. If you have partners in your life who are holding you back, you won't have room for positive partners who can offer you love and support. You can't have a relationship you want if you're holding onto a relationship you don't want.

If you have a partner whose lifestyle contradicts yours, you're going to have a very difficult time achieving your goals. For example, if you spend your weekends learning new skills to advance your career, training for competitions, or enjoying a creative hobby, and your partner wants to hang out around the house, drink beer, and play video games, their behavior might very well limit your ability to get where you want to be in life.

That's not to say people with different lifestyles and different goals are bad people—they just want something different in life than you want. The only way you can both get what you want may be by going in separate directions.

PARENT-CHILD RELATIONSHIPS

If you're a parent, consider how the relationships you model in front of your children affect them. Kids mirror their parents. If you settle for unhealthy relationships with people who hold you back from having the life you want, your children will grow up to settle for the same types of relationships.

If you show your children the value of good relationships with people who care about you and support you, your children will seek out similar relationships. When you settle for negative friendships, you're setting your kids up for unhappy relationships now and as they grow to become adults.

A high performance mindset allows you to engage in more positive relationships with your kids, because you're able to focus on them and be aware of their needs. Sometimes they need help with their homework and sometimes they need to be left alone. Sometimes they need your advice and sometimes they need you to listen. Sometimes kids just need a hug and to be told that everything will be okay. Unless you're tuned into them and paying attention, it's easy to make assumptions about what children need. However, by learning to control your focus and direct it toward them with active listening, you will be a better parent.

Your behavior toward your spouse, and how they treat you, teaches your child how to treat their own partners as they mature. If you're a dad and you treat your wife poorly, you're teaching your son to treat the women in his life the same way and/or you're teaching your daughter to accept that kind of treatment. Think hard about the relationships you model for your children, because they can have a profound effect on your kids' lives for many years.

Finally, be aware of how you treat everyone else in your life. Give people the benefit of the doubt and refrain from blaming other people for your problems. People aren't inherently bad or out to get you, and when you have children, you have to be particularly mindful of your attitude. Kids watch how you perceive and treat other people and they learn from your behavior. Hurt people, hurt people. When you see people lashing out, they are hurt themselves. Don't take it personally; find a way to help the situation.

CHAPTER

CRUSH YOUR GOALS

When you have a high performance mindset, you believe in yourself. You want more from yourself and you expect it. To get what you want out of life, you must set goals. That means choosing where you want to go in life. In a sense, you need to set your compass in the direction that will lead you to what you want to do, have, or be—your goals.

Think about your goals and what you may have to do in order to reach them. Are there obstacles in your way? Some people see obstacles as barriers to reaching their goals; however, remember, obstacles are nothing more than opportunities. If you have an obstacle in your way, you created it, thus, you can remove it by calling it an opportunity. This will challenge you in a positive way to ensure the obstacle is gone.

Have you ever been in an obstacle race? Did you get to a wall, some barbed wire, or a pool of mud and turn around? No, you probably scaled the wall, crawled under the wire, and slogged through the mud. Those obstacles gave you the opportunity to test your abilities. Without them, the obstacle race would have just been a race. Each obstacle became an opportunity to prove yourself. Life is the same way. Without obstacles, it would be a race to the finish line. You'd never get to test yourself or show off your abilities. If you see obstacles as barriers instead of opportunities, then that's your choice—you chose to make them barriers. They're not barriers unless you decide they are.

Seeing obstacles as opportunities is a different story. You can climb over them, crawl under them, or slog through them. You can knock them down. Obstacles are opportunities for challenging yourself on the way to reaching your goals. The goals are important because, without them, you wouldn't be motivated to continue. Why tackle the obstacles if there's no finish line? Without a target—an end in sight—there's no motivation to move forward.

In order for us to be motivated, we have to have a goal. Have you ever been motivated when you didn't have a goal? Everyone has goals; we just don't usually think of them as goals. Without certain goals, you wouldn't get out of bed in the morning. You get up because you're motivated to achieve your goal of going to work. Between getting out of bed and going to work you have smaller goals, like eating breakfast. Satisfying your hunger is the goal that motivates you to open the refrigerator and get some food. You take action throughout the day to achieve your many goals. Goals motivate you to do things that might be hard or uncomfortable, like overcoming challenges and accepting uncertainty. You get to that big wall on the course and you're not sure whether you can get over it. You give it your best shot—not knowing for sure whether you'll make it over the top or fall flat on your face—however, you accept that uncertainty because you have a goal. Goals help you to drive the direction your life takes, so you should put some real thought into the goals you set for yourself. They should mean something to you.

Goals typically fall into one of three categories: process goals, performance goals, and outcome goals. An *outcome goal* is what most people think about. It's something you want to achieve, like running your first 5K, becoming the director of your department, or starting your own business. However, people often neglect the work required to achieve that outcome, so they never reach that goal. Outcome goals take patience, planning, time and hard work. You can't run headlong toward an outcome goal and expect to reach it without putting in the work.

Process goals are the key to achieving your outcome goals. A process goal is achieved by mastering skills that allow you to reach an outcome. For example, if your outcome goal is to run a 5K, your process goal might be learning how to run with the proper gait, form, and speed. Process is the daily work—the grind, hustle, and effort—required to get you from where you are now to your outcome goal.

As you work on process goals, you should set *performance* goals. For example, if you start out running a mile in fifteen minutes, your goal might be to shave one minute off your time each week while slowly adding more distance to each run. Your performance goal for the second week would be running a mile in fourteen minutes, and in the third week your goal would be running a mile in thirteen minutes. As your running process improves, your performance will begin to improve. You'll reach your process goals, your performance goals, and—as you add more distance to your runs and increase your speed—you'll eventually achieve your outcome goal of running a 5K.

By focusing on the improvement of process work, outcome goals are achievable. You can run a 5K, a marathon, or a triathlon. You can get promoted or start your own business. When you're willing to put in the patience, planning, time and effort, anything is possible. However, if you want to run a 5K and you show up without first working on your process and performance goals, you probably won't finish.

Process work might be physical training or it might be education. It might be learning a new skill or getting better at something you already know how to do. Process goals always involve work—mental or physical—and that's how you develop and grow. With a high performance mindset, you'll be able to focus on process, improve your performance, and accomplish any outcome goals you set for yourself. Just remember, having a goal that requires more process work than you are willing to give will keep you from achieving that goal.

HOW TO SET A GOAL

For many, setting a goal can be quite the challenge.

As we mentioned earlier, you probably don't realize that you set goals every day. You set your alarm so that you get up when you're supposed to. When you're hungry, you set a goal to go eat. Some people feel that they're successful if they wake up and are able to place two feet on the ground. Their goal is to be able to get up every day. You really do set goals all the time. Consider this, though: How often do you intentionally set goals around what you want most in life? How often do you really think about your desired outcomes, and then identify the process and performance goals required to reach them?

Setting meaningful and powerful goals takes a bit of daydreaming. Too often, people feel that what they want is beyond their grasp, so they never even attempt to get it. We do this to protect ourselves. *That's too big...don't go for that. You will fail!* This happens to everyone to some extent. It's a protection mechanism and it hurts us. Everything around you, all that you can see with your eyes was created by someone who felt it was possible. You need to do the same thing. Imagine that the possibilities are limitless. What if you can have, do, or be anything. What would you wish for?

Write it down. Until you write it down, that thing you want is only a dream. Putting it down on paper makes it possible—a goal. Put your goals on sticky notes and place them where you'll see them every day. You can put them on the bottom of your computer screen, on your bathroom mirror, and on the dashboard of your car. You need to see your goals every day to remind yourself that's where you're headed. That goal is what you will someday have, do, or be.

As you develop your goals, ask yourself why you want them. Your *why* will greatly affect your odds of goal achievement.

If you're seeking an extrinsic reward, the chances of doing the work required to reach your goal aren't very good. However, if you're intrinsically motivated to achieve the goal, your odds of success are much better.

Here's what I mean by extrinsic and intrinsic rewards. Say you have a goal of going to the gym and getting in killer shape. *Why* do you want to get in shape? Ask yourself that question before you set that goal. If you want to get in shape so you can start dating good-looking men or women, you're seeking an extrinsic reward. You might be all gung-ho the first week you go to the gym, thinking about all the hot guys or gals you're going to be seeing. Then, after a week, you realize how hard it is to exercise. It takes a lot of effort and commitment, and you'd rather go home and eat dinner after work than go to the gym. You start to ask yourself if all that work is worth it. If you're getting in shape to please someone else, you probably won't stick with it long enough to make much of a difference in your appearance. However, let's say your doctor told you that you're at risk for heart disease and you can decrease your chances of health issues with regular exercise. He tells you to run on the treadmill for thirty minutes three times a week. Now you're going to be intrinsically motivated to exercise. There's an intrinsic reward that comes with reaching a goal like this—better health and less chance of heart disease. You could live longer and enjoy a better quality of life.

Intrinsic motivations and rewards are more powerful than those that are extrinsic. So, when you set your goals, ask yourself why you want to accomplish them. Identify the intrinsic motivation and reward, and if there isn't one, reconsider whether those goals are what you really want in life. What purpose will they serve?

While goals give you a target to shoot for, the path you take to reach them is more important. The journey you follow toward your process and performance goals—and ultimately, your outcome goals—is where you learn and grow. As you go through this journey and learn more, your outcome goals may very well change. Actually, this is quite common. We think we want something until we start heading toward it. We ultimately realize it may not be of interest anymore and because of what we've learned, we now have a new goal. For example, you may want to be in a certain position in your career. Maybe you want to be the director of your department. You figure out a process that will put you in the best position to be considered for that job and you follow the process. You might go back to school and get another college degree, or you might take some training and gain new skills. As you're going through the necessary process work, you discover that being the director of your department isn't everything you thought it was. So, you become interested in another position. As you learn and grow in the process of going after a goal, be open to changing your outcome goal. You set that initial goal with limited information, and as you go through the process, you'll learn more and your goals can shift.

On the other hand, you may actually accomplish your goal and decide it isn't what you wanted after all. Or, you meet the goal and then decide you want more—maybe you want to be the vice president of the department. You could discover another field along the way that interests you and decide you don't even want to pursue a career in your current department or industry. A lot can happen when you're pursuing a goal, and it's up to you to decide if the goal still makes sense or whether you'd be happier changing it.

If you're an athlete, you might have a goal of competing in a sprint triathlon, which is a half-mile swim, a 12.4-mile bike ride, and a 3.1-mile or 5K race. During the process of training for the race, you might become energized by the training, especially if you're seeing dramatic gains in your process and performance goals. Already, you're thinking about longer, more challenging races.

It's common for those who complete their first sprint triathlon to set a new outcome goal like competing in an Olympic-length triathlon, which is almost a mile swim followed by a 24.8-mile bike ride and a 6.2-mile race. You train for the race and find out that you can do this, and so you want more. After you compete, you sign up for a half Ironman Triathlon and, eventually, a full Ironman. Through the process of preparing and training for each consecutive race, you've improved your performance and realized that you want a new outcome goal. Suddenly, you're an Ironman Triathlete swimming 2.4 miles, biking 112 miles, and running a full marathon—26.2 miles—all in one day!

Remember, goals are about the journey. You evolve through the process, so be patient and be present. Goal achievement is taking a bunch of small actions and adjusting along the way—learning and applying, learning and applying. Achieving goals as quickly as you can is like building a house on a dirt foundation. As soon as it rains, your house will come crashing down!

GOALS AND THE "DOUBLE C" MINDSET

Working with athletes is truly a neat experience. Athletes are begging to go fast. Their bodies are in amazing shape; however, many athletes do not give enough attention to training their mind. One of the things I created to help athletes is called the "Double C!" This stands for Complete or Compete. With a complete mindset, your goal is to accomplish the outcome goal. You want to get across the finish line and, if you're in a race, you want to get across the finish line before the race ends. With a compete mindset, you take a competitive approach to the goal. You want to set a new personal best for yourself or perform better than anyone else who showed up that day. Maybe you want to be first in your age group or maybe you want to podium. If you have a compete mindset, you have to ramp up your process and performance goals. There's more work, more effort, and more intensity. You have to be more motivated to maintain a compete mindset.

Make sure your mindset matches your true goal. If the two aren't aligned, you won't be happy with your outcome. For example, if you tell yourself that you simply want to finish a race while, deep down, you really want to finish among the top ten in your age group, then make that your goal. If you don't, you won't do what's necessary to accomplish your true goal and you won't be happy with the outcome. If a goal seems beyond your reach, don't set a lower goal. We'll talk about this in more detail soon. Set your goal high and then set process and performance goals that will deliver your desired outcome. You can do it, as long as you're willing to do the work. Tough goals often take longer; however, the feeling of accomplishment will be worth its weight in gold.

This is especially important if you're working with a coach

in sports, a mentor at work, or a life coach in your personal life. Know what your true goals are and communicate them to the person whose job is supporting you so they can help you reach them. They need that information to help you succeed.

Goals and Visualization

As you will recall from Chapter 9, visualization is a powerful tool and it can help you achieve your goals. There is a huge gain from visualizing goal accomplishment! Imagine yourself crossing the finish line, getting that promotion, and making that successful speech. Visualizing the actualization of your goal primes your mind for the real thing. Remember, your brain processes the visualized version of your accomplishment as if it's the real thing. Have you ever practiced a speech, a run, or anything else that you're nervous about? That "dry run" prepared your body—and to a degree, your mind—for the actual event. Visualization prepares your mindset.

When you visualize your goal, use all your senses. Imagine how accomplishing that goal will look, sound, smell, taste, and feel. Play close attention to your emotions as you imagine your accomplishment. Do you feel excited? If you experience positive emotions during the visualization process, then you've chosen a good goal. If you do not, then put more thought into your goal. Is this really what you want?

After you visualize your goal, go a step further and draw a picture of it. Get out your crayons, colored pencils, or a pen and a notebook. You don't need to be an artist to do this—stick figures will do. Draw yourself reaching your goal. Look how happy you are! Now, hang that baby up where you can see it every day.

Don't be afraid to have goals. Don't shy away from the biggest, boldest goals you can fathom. Look around you. Everything you can see was, at some point, someone's dream. Someone thought it up and someone created it. This can be you. If you dream it, write it down, visualize it, and draw a picture of it—you'll start to realize that it's possible for you to reach it. Then step through the process necessary to get there.

GOAL SETTING MIND MAPPING

GOAL: *To buy a house*   **DATE TO COMPLETE:** *12/30/2017*

WHY DO YOU WANT THIS GOAL? HOW WILL IT MAKE YOU FEEL?
I have always wanted to own my own house. I would like to have a place I call mine instead of wasting money on rent. I would be so excited!

STEPS	POTENTIAL OPPORTUNITIES	DUE DATE
1. Call Bank and ask about credit score needed to get mortgage loan and ask about loan to income percentages	*Score is too low* *High credit usage*	*6/1/2017*
2. Pull a credit report and credit scores	*Inaccuracies in credit report* *Lower debt (will raise score)*	*6/1/2017*
3. Correct any errors in credit report		
4. Debt Management	*Might need more time*	*7/1/2017*
5. Check credit report again	*Usually takes 30 days to update*	*10/1/2017*
6. Gather all income information		*10/7/2017*
7. Go to lender and receive approval		*10/15/2017*
8. Shop and offer!	*Some may reject offers, keep looking*	*...*

Note: Potential Obstacles are reframed and entered under Potential Opportunities

DIAGRAM 11 - GOAL-SETTING MIND MAPPING

So, what's the process to reach my goal? That's a great question. Diagram 11, "Goal-Setting Mind Mapping," is an example of a goal and the process work you might follow to reach that goal. While you can use this template for any goal, in this example, the goal is to buy a house.

First, write down your goal and your deadline—the date by which you want to have accomplished your goal. Then write down *why* you want the goal. Here, the goal is to buy a house by December 30, 2017.

What will this goal do for you? How will it change your life and the lives of the people you care about? How will reaching this goal make you feel? Visualize it as you write it down.

Now you need to detail the process required to get the house. Buying a house seems like an enormous goal; however, once you break it down into steps, it becomes much more manageable. Remember, if you encounter a challenge, reframe it as an opportunity. For example, in this goal-setting mind map, the first thing you would do is call the bank to find out what your credit score should be to qualify for a home loan. You might discover that your credit score is too low because you have too much debt compared to your income. Instead of seeing that as a barrier, see it as an opportunity for you to lower your debt and raise your credit score. If you hadn't set the goal of buying the house, you wouldn't have called the bank, and you wouldn't be motivated to improve your credit. This is a good thing for you!

Set a date to get your credit score up to where it needs to be for that loan. Then schedule the next step: Pull a credit report. You can view your credit report online and look for potential errors and get them corrected. Also look for any reasons why your credit score is low. Do you have too much debt? Do you make late payments? Figure out what's affecting your credit and then follow the process to correct it. Three months later, your credit's in good shape and now you can take the next step of going to the bank and getting pre-approved for a home loan. Now you can call a real estate agent or start shopping around online for your house.

Although this seems simple, many people struggle with setting a big goal and reaching it, either because they think the goal is too lofty or because they give up at the first challenge. No goal is too big if you want it bad enough, and no challenge will keep you from reaching your goal if you see it as an opportunity. Change the way you think about life and your possibilities, and you'll be amazed by what you can accomplish.

FORMULATING, FOCUSING, AND ACHIEVEMENT

All your goals are reachable with a high performance mindset. You'll need that mindset to maintain the continuous action that's required to achieve them. Without action you're just daydreaming, so you have to put that mindset to work focusing on the goal and every step necessary to make it happen. You will have challenges. They're the steps you have to take to get where you're going.

Did you ever think about the fact that when you go to the store and buy something, you're getting a finished product? You don't see the thousands of hours of work that might have gone into developing and designing the prototypes of that product. You only see it in its finished state. Do you think someone built that thing exactly the way you see it on their first attempt? Remember when we talked about failure not being possible unless we quit? Well, Thomas Edison didn't quit as he searched for a way to create the light bulb. He attempted this feat thousands of times until he finally achieved his goal. He said, "I have not failed. I've just found 10,000 ways that won't work." He also said, "Many of life's failures are people who did not realize how close they were to success when they gave up." See? If you don't give up, Thomas Edison is telling you that you will not fail! Imagine how different the world would be if Edison had given up on the light bulb after one hundred attempts.

Your goals are no different. You can set a goal and move mountains to reach it if you want to. Don't think of it as a mountain—think of it as a big pile of rocks and each step in the process is a rock. You can move a rock. Don't get hung up thinking you're going to achieve your goal on the first attempt. In fact, if you accomplish your goal quickly and easily on the first attempt, then it probably wasn't a high enough goal to provide you with a lot of satisfaction.

As you work toward your goal, review the results to see whether you're moving in the right direction. You may have to readjust your process. Let's imagine a target one hundred yards from us and we have a little red laser. We get it ready and we shoot the laser toward the target. We don't hit it. What do we do? Well, we adjust. We move it a little bit to the right, and then we realize that wasn't the right direction. We adjust the laser to the left and we shoot it again. That didn't work either. We adjust it again. The thing about goals and life and failure is the fact that we need to recognize that it's a constant flow of small adjustments.

It's kind of like driving a car. Even if you're on a straightaway, you're always making tiny adjustments to keep your car aligned with the road and headed in the right direction. As long as you keep your foot on the gas and keep making those adjustments, you'll get there and you won't crash. Just don't stop. Stopping is giving up and that's the only way to fail at a goal. As long as you're taking action, you're making progress. You're learning and improving your process and reaching performance goals. All of that is bringing you closer to your desired outcome. As long as you're moving forward, you're learning, and that's never failure. Learning helps you dispel irrational thoughts, develop rational thoughts, and increase your ability to focus. It's how you keep your high performance mindset running on all four cylinders.

The number one reason that people don't chase after their goals is that they fear failure. People assume they can stay away from failure by never setting goals. Even though they could probably reach those goals, they are afraid to even shoot for them. You may not make your goal within the time limit you set for yourself; however, that's not failure—it's progress. Although you may not be promoted to the position you wanted, you'll learn a new skill and be closer to getting that position than you were before you set that goal. Even if you don't win the race, your time will improve and you'll finish. Attempting a goal and going through the process to reach it changes you, and that's progress. Let's say you're learning rifling. You aim your rifle at a target one hundred yards away. You line up your sight, pull the trigger, and you miss. What do you do? That's right, you adjust and shoot again. You don't quit. You go after it over and over again until you start hitting the target. This is not failing; this is learning and developing!

As long as you are willing to learn from each and every step in the process, adjust, and keep moving toward your goal, you can't fail. Now that you know you can't fail, you have nothing to fear and no reason to not set that goal for yourself—that pie-in-the-sky, fantastic goal that will make your life complete.

Be patient in your journey. Anything of value takes time to earn. If you don't believe this, look at your relationships. That love you have for someone took time to grow. Look at the work you did. You didn't wake up one day knowing how to do your job. Everything that you value—your relationships, education, skills and character—took time to build. It's easy to become impatient when you want something very badly. If you're losing weight and you look in the mirror every day, you'll feel like you aren't making progress because you don't see instant weight loss. It's the same with lifting weights to build muscle. You want to see results every day; however, bulking up takes time. It's the same with any goal worth having—they all take time and patience. If you continue working toward your goals and appreciate the progress you make with each step, you'll realize that you are moving forward—slowly. Be patient and don't quit. You'll get there.

Goals are like a road map. If you don't know the way from where you are to where you want to be, you can seek guidance from someone who's already reached that goal. For example, if you want to be a CEO, talk to CEOs and ask them what they did to get into those positions. Someone you know *knows* a CEO or *is* a CEO. Find that person, call them up, and ask if you can have some time to speak with them. You don't need to spend the whole day together—just a few minutes to explain where you are and your goal. Find out what your next step should be. You don't need them to draw you a map, just to give you their advice on which direction to take right now. Once you've taken that step, the next step might be obvious. If it isn't, call him again and ask him for advice on your next step. Don't be a pest and call him every day—he's busy. Be clear about where you are and what you need to know. If he can respond to you in a few minutes or with a few sentences in an email, he'll probably be happy to help you. You can also read a book that tells you how to reach your specific goal. Educate yourself. The library's free.

Every step you take toward your goal is a tiny success. Have you ever heard the phrase "fail yourself to success?" That's a ridiculous idea, because whatever you do to reach your goal isn't a failure no matter how bad the outcome. You're still making progress and there's nothing to fear. There are no dead ends on your map, because you didn't put any there.

People who are the most successful at reaching their goals

are able to delay their gratification. If you're patient and can wait for the payoff, you'll be more likely to commit the time and effort needed to work through the process. If you realize along your path to your goal that the original goal you set no longer has any value, change it. Change your goal to something that does matter and divert your progress and your momentum toward that new goal. Motivation isn't something you can create out of thin air. Motivation is driven by goals. If you want to learn how to be motivated, set a goal for yourself that's of value. Do your homework and develop a process for reaching it. Set process and performance goals, and take the first step. The motivation will appear like magic.

REACHING YOUR GOALS REQUIRES MAKING CHOICES

The daily choices you make will either move you closer to your goals or further away from them. You'll have to make the right choices to get what you want, and some of them will be hard. They won't be comfortable; however, remember that getting what you want isn't supposed to be easy. It is doable, though, and you can do this.

What happens if you're surrounded by people who keep you from your goals? Over time, your friendships may change. If your friends want something different than you do, they may not want to hang out with you anymore. You may decide your time is better spent alone or with other people. These choices can be hard; however, life isn't about doing what's easy or convenient. Your high performance mindset is built to focus on the thoughts that drive actions that take you where you want to go, not built to get you pushed around by what other people want. Your goals, lifestyle, and relationships have to be aligned.

YOU CAN'T HAVE A PLAN B

Plan A is the goal you really want. Some people have a Plan B. Plan A might be their parachute and Plan B is the safety net that's going to catch them if the parachute doesn't open. If you have a safety net, how committed are you to learning how to jump out of a plane? How much do you care about how well the parachute's packed? You won't be committed at all if there's a net to catch your fall. Plan B destroys your motivation to reach Plan A. If your focus moves to Plan B, you can't be focused on Plan A anymore, and you will never achieve that goal. Remember, you can only focus on one thought at a time, and you can only focus on one plan for reaching your goal at a time. You can change your goal—your Plan A—if you decide it's no longer what you want; however, don't rely on a safety net. If you decide Plan A isn't for you, change it. Come up with a new Plan A.

That's not to say that you should only have one goal. You can have many different goals, and be in different stages of reaching them. Once you accomplish a goal, have another goal in progress so you can keep up your momentum. If you don't have more than one goal, think about what will happen when you accomplish the goal you currently have. For example, if your only goal is to complete an Ironman, you're going to train hard for six months or longer until you finally compete. You might have a spectacular time in the Ironman. After the race is over, what happens? Well, since you don't have another goal waiting in the wings, you could get really bummed out. For months, you've been looking forward to the Ironman and now that it's over, you have nothing to look forward to. I call this the post-Ironman blues and it's more common than you think. Instead, if you race in May and you have a second goal lined up—maybe competing in another Ironman in August—then you can take a short break after your first race and jump right into training for the next one. These goals can build on each other, and as you achieve one, that goal can set you up for greater success in the next one. If you've ever reached a goal and felt depressed afterward, you probably didn't have another goal to look forward to. So, as you're working toward a major goal, think ahead about what you'll want to accomplish next.

Use the goal-setting mind map as a template for setting

your goals and setting up the process to reach them. Make sure you have at least two goals all the time. They could be sports goals, career goals, or personal goals like buying a house. For example, you might be training for a sprint marathon while looking ahead to running a half, so the processes for those goals will build on each other. If you're an executive, you probably have many goals. Your leadership has goals that they want you to focus on to help them meet their goals, and you have your own goals for yourself, your employees, and your department.

Those goals can also build on each other. For example, maybe your CFO wants you to cut hiring costs. You know that whenever an employee leaves your department, it costs a lot of time and money to hire and train a replacement. Reducing attrition—say, by decreasing the number of people who leave your department annually by 50 percent—would be an excellent goal that would satisfy your CFO. That's one goal. Part of that goal might be increasing employee engagement. If your employees have interesting work that contributes to the company's success, you know they'll be more engaged and less likely to leave your department. Your goal for your employees, then, is to figure out how to get them more engaged in their work. That's another goal. You decide that you need to learn how to create a survey for your employees, so taking a quick course in survey building and employee engagement might be a personal career goal for you. Each of these goals requires a separate set of steps, and they build on each other and contribute to the overall success of you, your employees, your department, and your CFO.

When you're looking to make improvements—whether it's in a sport, your personal life, or at work—look at what's already working. Look for the successes and the successful people behind them. Talk to those people and find out what they're doing. While it's human nature to focus on the weaknesses and attempt to fix them, you can only focus on one thing at a time. Look for your strengths and dedicate yourself to them. Keep building on them. If you focus solely on your weaknesses, your strengths will weaken, too. You can't ignore the weaknesses and hope they'll go away. Instead, look outside yourself for help with them. You have your strengths and there is someone in your life or at work who is very good at whatever it is that you're struggling with. Enlist their help and focus your own energies on what you do well. When everyone dedicates themselves to their strongest talents, the whole organization improves.

CHAPTER

UNLOCKING YOUR PURPOSE WITH THE HIGH PERFORMANCE MINDSET

How many times have you asked yourself, "Why am I here? Everyone says we have a purpose; however, I don't know what mine is."

If you've asked yourself that question, you'll find this very helpful. Do you remember the tank man back in the 1980s? The tank man stood in front of a long line of Chinese military tanks to stop their progress. The picture of him was one of the most powerful, iconic photographs ever published. When you saw that picture, did you envision yourself being a person who makes that kind of impact with your life?

How about the story of Rosa Parks? She was told to move to the back of the bus, yet she refused to get up. She took a stand for what she felt was right. Think about movies you've seen that affected you and how you looked at life, like *A Walk to Remember*, *Lincoln Lawyer*, *The Pursuit of Happiness*, *Gran Torino*, *300*, *Hotel Rwanda*, and even *Taken*. All of these movies have one common thread: They're heroic stories. We admire heroes for their bravery on screen and often envision ourselves doing what they have done. These heroes didn't have special powers. They were ordinary people who did extraordinary things. They chose to act. The power of possibility we see in the acts of heroes inspires us and can even cause us to respond emotionally at times. Being heroic requires selflessness and nobility. We all have this ability.

Heroes do what must be done. They don't think about it—they act. There are people who stand up for what's right, regardless of their fears, like the tank man. People relate to everyday heroes on a very deep level, because they remind us that we have a purpose in life and are here for a reason. We relate to heroic movies and stories because, deep down, we want to be a hero to others. Heroes give to something greater than themselves. They don't commit heroic acts for fame or fortune. They're selfless and they put others first, because it's the right thing to do and subconsciously, that desire to do what's right connects us all together.

Think about all the times you've helped people through hard times. Maybe you bathed a best friend who was hurt in a car wreck or pulled over to help someone change their tire. Maybe you gave someone a dollar when they were short. You've probably donated time or money to the needy or taken a meal to a friend who lost a loved one. Those were heroic actions. Heroes drive connectedness and increase our overall positivity. That is what high performance mindsets do. These actions may not seem like much to you; however, to the people they serve, they are heroic.

Your purpose in life is to be a hero. You can do this by using your own personal growth, development, and experience to help those in need. You can give back to them and to society. Being a hero to someone is intrinsically motivating because you get an immediate reward—that amazing feeling you get when you know you've made a positive difference in the life of another human being. You have so much to offer the world and you can be a hero every single day.

Now that you know your purpose, look at your personal and professional goals. Is there a connection between your purpose and your goals? Many people don't make the connection between their everyday lives and their actual purpose for being here, and that can be extremely demotivating. Not knowing why you do what you do can lead to disengagement. Whatever you do, figure out how you can use your skills, education, and experience to be someone's hero. This will help you tie your purpose to your life and your work. No matter what you do, you can be helping someone. Focus on the helping part instead of the job part.

If you're a training coach, you're a hero to the athletes you push to limits they never thought were possible. If you're a mechanic, your purpose—your act of heroism—is helping someone gain their freedom by fixing their car. If you're a nurse, your heroism is helping your patients get well while comforting their family. If you're a cashier at a local supermarket, you may not realize the customer you're working with has a horrible home life and they hate their job. By asking them about their day and showing that you care, you can become their hero. All it takes is asking one simple question and then paying attention to the response. You never know; you may be the only person who's asked them how they are in a long time. Maybe you're a call center employee. Customers don't call you asking about the weather. They call because they need your help. You're their hero when you empathize with them and resolve their issue. Even if they're angry or frustrated, listening to them vent is an act of heroism, because you're using your powers of patience to allow them to be heard. Eventually, they'll regain their composure and then you can use your powers of problem-solving to remedy their problem. They might even call you their hero in the end.

As I've mentioned previously, people often think they're in the banking business, health care business, food industry, or sales. The truth is, everyone in any industry is in the people business. Work is about relationships and connectedness. Look at your own career and think about how you serve people. Recognize that your purpose in life is to be someone's hero, to help them out, and to give back to a greater good. Look at your role and focus on how it helps others. If you focus on this part of your position, you'll find happiness in any job.

In your personal life, you can be a hero by donating blood or bone marrow, by being an organ donor, and by donating time or money to a charity. Be someone's hero today and every day. Live that life of purpose. Focus on that goal in everything you do, and you'll receive more in return than you could ever imagine. The feeling you get being a hero is the biggest payoff you'll ever receive. Being a hero, satisfying your main purpose, is possible by living your life with that one goal in mind.

CELEBRATE THE PROCESS

In the pursuit of your goals, it's natural to focus on the

goals themselves and lose sight of the process. However, the process—the patience, planning, time, and effort you put toward your goals—are the real successes and they are what determine your actual progress and growth. Remember to pause every now and then to take a breath, look back, and appreciate how far you've come. There's a good chance you've come a long way and are closer to a goal that you once believed was impossible. Think about where you started from and compare that to where you are right now. Incredible, isn't it? Can you imagine, with all the progress you've made, what's possible for you in the future? It's astounding. You are capable of so much.

Looking back at your development gives you a clear idea of how successful you really are. If you simply focus on the outcome goal, you'll spend a lot of time feeling like you're not getting anywhere. The fact is, each day, every action you take and step you make in the process is a victory.

THE FINISH LINE

So here we are—the last chapter. I'm very proud of you for reading this book, and I already know you'll be successful because of the dedication you have put into it. If there's *one* lesson I want you to come away with, it's this: Change is certain and the high performance mindset recognizes change as good. Once you accept change as an opportunity to better your own life and the lives of other people, you realize what a gift change is.

The most important step you take is the next one. Although you can't control next week, next month, or next year, you have a lot of control over what you do with the next moment of your life. Your mind is always learning, growing, and evolving, and you have a choice in what it becomes and the direction it takes your life. There are a lot of exercises, tools, and lessons in this book, and you may have to read it several times to remember everything and be able to apply all the tools. As you read through the book again, start doing the exercises. Do them every day. Bookmark those pages so you can get to them quickly, and then write down your ABCDE exercises, your affirmations, and your goals. Practice visualization. Use it to prepare yourself for upcoming challenges and to prepare your mind to achieve your goals.

This book is fully loaded with what you need to build the high performance mindset; however, you have to act. Take action. Don't just read this book, close it, and then put it on the shelf. That's what most people do. You spent hours reading this book—take advantage of what you've learned. The high performance mindset is possible when you act. Then everything is possible.

IT'S TIME TO TAKE THE WHEEL

Living life to the fullest, simply put, is living a happy life. Everything is easier when you're happy. Yet many people choose to live in unhappy circumstances. They choose to date and marry people who treat them badly, choose to work in positions that limit their abilities and happiness, and choose to live a life of fear and worry.

Notice how I used the word *choose*, as though living with

unhappiness is a choice. If it was a choice, why would anyone choose to live an unhappy life? People make choices out of habit. Their subconscious mind likes patterns and their conscious mind likes to repeat its thoughts. While a lot of those patterns and thoughts are negative, the key to overcoming them is recognizing them for what they are and making the *choice* to change them. The key to *your* happiness is unlocking the possibilities that exist beyond those habits, patterns, and repeating thoughts. There is so much more to life; and, once you unlock the possibilities, you can generate a new story for your life, a story of happiness.

You have all the tools you need to build your own high performance mindset and now it's up to you to do the work. Look at where you are in the car. Are you in the passenger seat? Get in the driver's seat and take the wheel. Remember that the only way to fail is to quit. Put the pedal to the metal and keep driving forward.

You can make a difference in this world every single day. However, you have to start right now. Don't wait until you get a new job, lose weight, get stronger, or get married to develop a high performance mindset. And don't wait for it to get warmer or for the sun to come out, and most importantly, don't put off the work I've outlined in this book until tomorrow. Every unhappy moment you accept is gone from your life and you can never get it back. You will not get a do-over in this moment or in any other moment going forward. This is your life, and right now is the perfect time to take control of it.

Choose to love and invest in yourself. Choose not to compare yourself to others or worry about what they think of you. Choose to accept where you are, knowing that you can go anywhere from here with the right mindset. Choose to give to others and be a hero for someone every day for the rest of your life.

Be grateful for what you have and the world will become a different place. The high performance mindset is contagious and, as you change your thoughts and your life, you'll change the lives of those around you.

All the exercises in this book—and more—can be found at thehighperformancemindset.net (password THPM) and if you need more guidance, you can find me at craigwillard.com on Facebook and Instagram at /CraigWillardCoaching. Reach out to me and let me know how you're doing. Tell me about the struggles and the successes. If you know someone who could benefit from the high performance mindset, loan them this book or buy them a copy. Invite them to visit my website, Instagram, or Facebook page—I'd love to hear from them, too.

ABOUT THE AUTHOR

 **CRAIG WILLARD** is a certified high performance coach, leadership coach, new life story coach, mental sports coach, and a member of the International Coaching Federation and the Association for Applied Sports Psychology. He is a Ph.D. candidate who has leveraged his psychology research and real-world coaching experience into a transformative program for improving your thought processes. His high performance mindset techniques have been successfully tested by executives, athletes, and everyday people who wanted more out of their lives. Visit Craig at craigwillard.com for more information.

Made in the USA
Lexington, KY
16 August 2017